THE ROUGH GUIDE to the

iPad

by

Peter Buckley

ROUGH GUIDES

www.roughguides.com

Credits

The Rough Guide to the iPad

Text and design: Peter Buckley
Editing and layout: Kate Berens
Proofreading: Jason Freeman
Production: Rebecca Short

Rough Guides Reference

Director: Andrew Lockett
Editors: Kate Berens, Peter Buckley,
Tracy Hopkins, Matthew Milton,
Joe Staines, Ruth Tidball

Publishing information

This first edition published July 2010 by
Rough Guides Ltd, 80 Strand, London, WC2R 0RL
Email: mail@roughguides.com

Distributed by the Penguin Group:
Penguin Books Ltd, 80 Strand, London, WC2R 0RL
Penguin Group (USA), 375 Hudson Street, NY 10014, USA
Penguin Group (Australia), 250 Camberwell Road, Camberwell, Victoria 3124, Australia
Penguin Group (Canada), 90 Eglinton Avenue East, Suite 700, Toronto, Ontario, Canada M4P 2Y3
Penguin Group (New Zealand), Cnr Rosedale and Airborne Roads, Albany, Auckland, New Zealand

Printed and bound by Legoprint, Italy
Typeset in Minion and Myriad
iPad hardware and software images courtesy of Apple

The publishers and author have done their best to ensure the accuracy and currency of all information in *The Rough Guide to the iPad*; however, they can accept no responsibility for any loss or inconvenience sustained by any reader as a result of its information or advice.

256 pages; includes index

A catalogue record for this book is available from the British Library.

ISBN 13: 978-1-84836-893-4

1 3 5 7 9 8 6 4 2

For Caroline and Rosalie

Contents

Part 6: Pictures

Part 7: Communicating

Part 8: Contacts and calendars

Part 9: The World Wide Web

Part 10: Navigation

Part 11: Productivity

Part 12: Accessories

Introduction

A lot of people asked me why I was writing a book on the iPad. Surely there's not enough to say, now that everyone's so used to iPods and iPhones? And what about the Internet? Isn't everything we need to know available online?

And yet, many of these same people followed on with a rally of questions about the device. Does it feel heavy to hold? What's the score with the non-replaceable battery? Should I go for the Wi-Fi or 3G model?

There's lots of misinformation about, and rather than filtering through all the "noise" of the Internet, people wanted a one-stop shop for answers, advice and suggestions. That's what I hope you'll be getting here: a couple of hundred pages of tips, tricks and answers to all those nagging questions that pop up before you buy a device like the iPad, and when you turn the thing on for the first time. And then answers to a whole bunch of questions that you didn't even know you wanted to ask in the first place.

What about the iPad itself? Like the iPod and iPhone, the iPad looks set to revolutionize the way people think about their digital lifestyles. It's the device that cements the idea that computing isn't just about number-crunching, mice and keyboards, but is about the things we do every day around the home and out and about. Just think about the possibilities for this kind of device: it offers a whole new way to enjoy the Internet; you can prop it up in the kitchen to follow a recipe; relax in bed with a favourite novel or the latest news; show photos to friends in the pub; tap out a few emails; even knock out a spreadsheet. The list is seemingly endless, and it isn't hard to imagine a not-too-distant future where there are a couple of iPads lying around every home.

The fact that you're reading this shows you're interested in the iPad. You may well have bought one already. You might even be reading this on its screen (just as I am writing this on its screen). For a moment, however, let's assume you're one of the many people who don't get what all the fuss is about. Well, it's an Apple product for a start, and that's reason enough to make a fuss in some circles. Apple don't tend to release a new product unless the time is right and the experience is absolutely cracking. The time is most certainly right for a reinvention of the personal computer, and touchscreen technology (like that found in most smartphones these days) is proving itself the undisputed successor to the mouse and keyboard.

So, what to expect when you get the iPad out of the box for the first time? Well, after the initial "wow" moment, expect a couple of days of mild confusion... It isn't necessarily obvious how this device is going to fit into your daily life. But any doubts soon pass as you find yourself using the iPad more and more – and that's where this book will help, hooking you up with the best apps and showing you all the tips and tricks you need to discover where the iPad fits into your own or your family's life.

If there's one thing that you'll learn during these first few weeks, it's that the iPad is a blank canvas, and with the right apps installed, the possibilities are limitless... Enjoy.

About this book

Text written like **this** denotes a command or label as it appears on either a computer's screen or the iPad's screen. Something written like **this** refers to the name of an app that can be downloaded from the Apple App Store.

This book was written using a first-generation iPad running iPhone OS 3.2. (To see which version of the software you're running, connect your iPad to iTunes, highlight it in the iTunes sidebar, and then click the Summary tab.) If you're running a later version of the OS then you may well come across features not covered here, though the majority of what's written will still apply.

Acknowledgements

Thanks go to Kate Berens, Andrew Lockett and everyone at Rough Guides who helped get this book together in record time. Also to Duncan, Joe and Jonathan for their camaraderie and a special shout to Therese Burke and Robert Stillman – I couldn't have done it without you. Thanks also to Caroline and Natasha for use of their pop promos in the video player shots, and also to all the developers whose efforts are mentioned in these pages. And a special thanks to my wife and daughter for their endless supply of encouragement, coffee and toast.

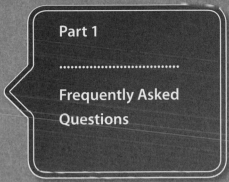

Part 1

....

Frequently Asked Questions

What you need to know...

...but were afraid to ask

The big picture

What's an iPad?

In Apple's eye, the iPad is the missing link between the iPhone and their MacBook (laptop) range. It's a tablet computer that offers the best of both worlds: the touch screen and breadth of activities of a smartphone (web browsing, email, etc), but with a size and computing power verging on that of some laptops. It can also play music, movies and video and display eBooks. Add to this the ability to play videogames and install applications (or apps), and you have a pretty impressive device.

After months of speculation, the iPad was launched in April 2010 in the US and then in the UK and elsewhere soon after. First on the scene was a Wi-Fi-only version, which was swiftly followed by a slightly pricier model with both Wi-Fi and 3G connectivity.

Is the iPad the first device of this kind?

Tablet computers (flat computing devices with an interactive screen making up the majority of one face) are not new, but this is the first time that such a device has really captured the public imagination and showed the potential to become a mainstay of the computing world.

At this point it is worth mentioning the recent growth of eBook readers and the particular success of devices such as Amazon's Kindle and the Sony Reader – various models of slim, tablet-like device that allow you to read book content on, to date, a black-and-white, easy-on-the-eye, E Ink screen (more on this later). Though more often than not single-function devices, without a touch screen or colour, eBook readers have set the scene for the appearance of the iPad, which in turn, will very probably bury them.

The Apple Newton

Long before the iPad, or even the iPod, showed its face, there was the Newton... Apple's first venture into the world of tablet computing. The project kicked off in 1989, and for the next decade the various Newton incarnations wholeheartedly failed to capture the public's imagination, though they did find a home amongst a select set of business users. Unlike the iPad, the Newtons used a stylus rather than a finger for input, and also featured handwriting recognition technology (sadly missing as a built in feature of the first-generation iPads). By the end of the 1990s, the Newton project had been terminated, but its influence remained and the years since have witnessed near-constant speculation about when Apple would again embrace tablet computing.

How does it compare to the iPhone and iPod Touch?

Well, for a start, it's bigger, both in terms of physical dimensions and storage capacity. At the time of writing, for example, Apple iPhones are available with capacities of either 8, 16, or 32GB of storage space (less around 1GB, which accounts for the operating system, or OS). The first iPads shipped with 16, 32 or 64GB (again, with around 1GB taken up by the OS).

However, it is more interesting to see what characteristics the iPad shares with its smaller siblings. The main similarity comes in the software and user interface: all run on versions of the same operating system and use the same touch-screen technology. From Apple's perspective, this system works brilliantly. It means that iPhone apps will run on the iPad straight out of the box (more on this below), but even more significantly, it means that there are millions of people out there who are already familiar with the interface that appears on the iPad. And when you tot up all the iPhone and iPod Touch users in the world, that's a lot of potential iPad customers.

So for many, moving to the familiar interface and OS of the iPad will be a very easy transition, while the added screen size (it measures 9.7 inches diagonally, compared to the 3.5 inches of the iPhone screen) allows for many interesting twists to the user experience that those accustomed to the iPhone and iPod Touch already know and love.

To quickly sum it up, the merits of the iPad, besides its slick design, include:

• A huge, bright, high-resolution (1024x768 pixels) screen with a resolution of 132 pixels per inch, which changes orientation when you rotate the iPad.

• A responsive touch-screen interface that can be understood by almost anyone in a matter of seconds

• A built-in digital compass and location-aware technology (aka "assisted GPS").

• An intuitive, user-friendly software system.

• An excellent web browser and a top-class email application

• Compatibility with iTunes on a Mac or PC for syncing content and data.

- Wi-Fi (in all models) and 3G capability (in some models) for fast Internet access.

- Loads of downloadable games and applications.

- Gigabytes of storage space for movies, music, photos, eBooks and more.

And how big is it overall?

The Wi-Fi-only model weighs in at 0.68kg (1.5 pounds), while the Wi-Fi+3G version is 0.78kg (1.6 pounds) – that's roughly about the same as the average hardback novel. Looking at the iPad head-on it measures a touch under 189mm (7.47 inches) wide and just under 243mm (9.56 inches) tall. Looking from the side, it's about 13mm (half an inch) at its thickest point, which tapers down to a quarter of an inch at the edges. Visit apple.com/ipad/specs for more detailed specifications.

Why did Apple skimp on the screen and not make it stretch right to the edges?

Like on the iPhone and iPod Touch you mean? Put simply, you have to be able to hold the thing, and the black bevel around the edge gives you somewhere to put your thumbs without obscuring content or confusing the device with unnecessary taps and swipes.

Can I use a stylus instead of my finger?

To get technical for a moment, the iPad's screen recognizes your touches in terms of the very specific electrical capacitance of your fingers, and not the actual pressure of your finger as you tap or swipe (as would be the case with most stylus touch systems). That said, there is one stylus device on the market designed specifically for iPhones, iPods and the iPad. It's called the Pogo Sketch and you can find out more at tenonedesign.com/sketch.php.

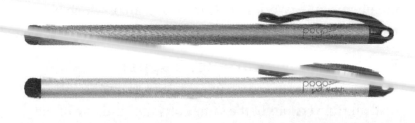

The other, slightly wackier solution, popular in Korea amongst iPhone users, is to employ a particular brand of snack sausage which displays similar electrostatic characteristics as the human finger – perfect for cold days when you don't want to take your gloves off. For the full story, visit tinyurl.com/yldwb38.

What software can I expect to find on my new iPad?

Straight out of the box, the iPad features several apps that will be familiar to anyone who has owned an iPod Touch or iPhone. There's Mail, Photos, Notes, Calendar, Contacts, Maps and YouTube (no prizes for guessing what any of those do) and also Safari (Apple's excellent web browsing application). The iPad also comes with a built-in iPod app (for music and other audio content) and a Videos app, for playing back movies, TV shows and other video content. Though familiar, all of these applications have been reworked to make the best use of the available screen size that the iPad boasts.

Apple have also built several other excellent iPad apps including Remote (see p.131), iBooks (see p.106) and the members of the iWork suite (see p.231), all of which have to be downloaded separately from the iTunes App Store.

So, the iPad can run iPhone apps?

As already mentioned, the iPhone, iPod Touch and the iPad all run versions of the same software, and one of the upshots of this is that pretty much all applications found in the iTunes App Store will also run on the iPad. However, it's worth understanding the distinction between apps that are designed to work on iPads and smaller-screen devices (and present a different interface, depending on the device) and those that were built for the iPod Touch or iPhone and run on the iPad scaled-up to fit nearly all of the screen (pictured below) using the iPad's 2x mode.

Scaled apps are not always ideal. Firstly, the graphics can end up looking rather chunky (because each pixel within the app has had its real estate quadrupled), but also, the actual layout of many apps (designed for a pocket-sized device) can seem very odd on the larger screen – especially with regard to simpler, one-function apps, where once finger-sized buttons bloat to fill half the screen, leaving you feeling like a diminutive Alice after a sip from the "Drink Me" bottle.

It will be interesting to see how this situation plays out, given the alternatives available to developers. The expectation is that many developers will look to create a separate version of their existing apps for the iPad or create a version that works on both.

So, basically, any app is going to work?

Not necessarily. Keep in mind that some apps popular on the iPhone utilize either its cellular call features or the device's camera (for example, those that employ "augmented reality" to display information overlaying a real-time image), and given that the first-generation iPad ships sans-camera, and can't be used to make cellular calls, certain apps will be about as useful as a chocolate kettle.

How many apps can I load onto the iPad?

As with the iPhone and iPod Touch, the iPad can accommodate multiple Home Screens. You can have up to eleven of them, and each holds up to twenty icons. The Dock at the bottom of the Home Screen houses another six (the same six across each Home Screen), which gives a grand total of 226. This number includes both the built-in application icons that you can't remove and any web-clip icons that you might have added (see p.70).

As for data storage capacity, you shouldn't have any problem filling all 226 slots, as the majority of apps are relatively small. To see how much of your iPad's capacity is accounted for by apps, connect to iTunes, highlight the device in the left-hand panel and take a look at the multi-coloured status panel at the bottom of the Summary pane (pictured below).

As it's made by Apple, will it also run Mac applications?

No, it's a completely different system that requires applications to be designed with Multi-Touch interactivity in mind. That said, many developers who build apps for desktop and laptop Mac machines are creating iPad versions of their more popular applications.

Connectivity questions

Can I make voice or video phone calls with it?

Video calls are currently a no no, as the iPad has no camera, let alone a front-facing one (like the iSight cameras on Apple MacBooks). If this omission is a deal-breaker for you, then hold out for a future model, which is sure to come, at some point, with the extra hardware.

As for voice calls, the iPad does feature a built-in microphone and a single mono speaker (the headphone output jack is stereo), so calls are possible using VoIP (Voice over Internet Protocol) services such as Skype, which allow you to connect to other VoIP users and traditional landlines via the Internet.

Don't be fooled into thinking you can use the device as a cellphone by the existence of the 3G-enabled iPad. This model does allow you to connect to a phone operator's network, but these connections are for data transfers only (emails, web browsing, etc) not cellular calls or SMS.

Can you tell me more about the iPad's connectivity?

All iPad models have built-in support for Bluetooth and Wi-Fi. More specifically, they support the current fastest Wi-Fi standard: 802.11n. Wi-Fi standards are backwards compatible, so you should have no issues connecting to Wi-Fi networks that support the older 802.11b and 802.11g standards, although early iPad adopters did run into these

3G, EDGE and GPRS... what's all that about?

Over time, the technology used to transmit and receive data using mobile devices has improved, allowing greater range and speed. Of the network technologies widely available at present, 3G (third generation) is the most advanced, allowing Internet access at speeds comparable to home broadband connections.

Unsurprisingly, it's this speedy 3G standard that the 3G-compatible iPad models use to supply a data connection when there are no Wi-Fi networks available. You'll know you're connected, as "3G" will appear alongside the signal indicator bars on the iPad's Status Bar at the top of the screen. At other times, however, you may see "EDGE" appearing on the Status Bar instead. EDGE (or Enhanced Data rates for GSM Evolution, to give it its rather grand full name) is a slower standard of data network (sometimes referred to as "2.75G"), which is more widely available in non-urban areas than 3G. You'll find when connected to EDGE that browsing the web is far slower, but battery life better, than over 3G. EDGE offers a theoretical top speed of 236 kilobits per second (kbps); in practice, however, users have more often than not experienced data rates as slow as 50kbps – like an old-fashioned dial-up connection.

Slower still is the GPRS standard, which is represented by a ° icon on the iPad's Status Bar.

exact problems during the first few weeks of the iPad's release. Unless you encounter any specific issues with a particular home network setup, there is no need to worry about all these different standards, as they can generally all coexist happily.

The 3G version of the iPad also includes a SIM card tray, which houses a special 3G SIM card. 3G is a data standard used by many cellphone network providers to handle the ever-growing data demands of their customers. If you suspect that you are largely going to use your iPad at home and connect via Wi-Fi you may well not need the option of a 3G connection. If, however, you are looking to employ your iPad in the wider world – on the commute to work, say – then it's well worth considering. For more on these options, turn to p.48.

Can I "unlock" the iPad and use my current cellphone's SIM card and network?

When the iPhone was first launched, each purchased device was "locked" to a specific network. Naturally, it didn't take geeks long to figure out how to "unlock" the iPhone's software for use with any SIM card and network. The downsides were that unlocking invalidated your Apple warranty, and certain unlocking solutions also disabled some functions and made it impossible (or risky) to install software updates from Apple.

So to answer your question with regard to the iPad: there's some good news and some bad. The good news is that in the majority of territories the 3G iPad comes officially unlocked, which means that you can choose which network provider you want to go with, without having to worry about invalidating your warranty or messing with the software.

But before you go and crack open your cellphone to get at the SIM, here's the bad news. The iPad uses a special micro-SIM card (also known as a 3FF SIM), so the one you currently use won't fit. What's more, there aren't that many network providers yet offering the micro-SIM, which will, at least for a while, seriously limit your choice of network.

Can I get my iPad online by tethering it to my iPhone?

Tethering is the process whereby one device connects to the Internet via the online connection of another device. So, for example, with the right data plan you can employ an iPhone, say, as a wireless modem for a laptop. The situation may well change in certain territories in the future, but, at the time of writing, tethering an iPad is not possible.

Can I use the iPad overseas?

When it comes to foreign use of web, email, maps and other Internet-based features, you're best sticking to Wi-Fi hotspots where you can get online for free (or pay a reasonable charge for access). In many countries it's possible to connect via the local 3G phone networks if you have a 3G-capable iPad, but be prepared for some really savage fees. If you can stomach the costs, turn Data Roaming .... ithin Settings > Cellular Data. Perhaps the best solution is to purchase a compatible ... ... SIM locally when you go abroad and then access the data networks at the local rate.

Does the iPad feature a GPS system?

The Wi-Fi+3G model includes an actual GPS (Global Positioning System) chip. Similar to the iPhone 3GS, it offers so-called "Assisted GPS", which means it combines satellite positioning data with cellular network data (a triangulation of the nearest network masts) and also any available Wi-Fi network data. The Wi-Fi-only model does not contain a GPS chip, and so relies on connected Wi-Fi networks to determine its position.

Will these "location services" work overseas without costing me a fortune in roaming charges?

It's worth noting that the digital compass and location-aware features *can* operate independently of data roaming. So as long as you use an app with "offline" mapping features (i.e., the map data is downloaded as part of the app, and not pulled from the Internet as and when it is needed), you should be able to get a fix on your current location using a Wi-Fi+3G iPad with roaming off.

iPad vs Macs and PCs

What should I go for as a secondary computing device: an iPad or a netbook?

The iPad can't run the same versions of the application you use on a PC, and it doesn't have a conventional file and folder system like Windows does. Conventional input and output ports, such as USB and LAN, are also missing, as is a CD/DVD drive. Critics routinely point out that the iPad does not support Adobe's Flash media format, which is required to view content on many popular web sites. Lack of an integrated hardware keyboard is also a common complaint. Finally, it's worth noting the price differential too, as you will pay a premium (often referred to as the "Apple Tax") for the quality and design of Apple products.

All that said, netbooks and other diminutive laptops also have their issues. The two killers being the frustratingly small keyboards and screens, and also the fact that they more often than not don't boast the processing power they should to deal with fully fledged operating systems. The end result is a slow and clunky experience. Google are currently addressing these issues with the release of their stripped-down Chrome OS – a lightweight operating system with cloud computing services (rather than traditional applications) at its heart. It's an interesting option and worth a look.

As for the choice between the iPad and a netbook, it's really down to personal preference. With regard to Apple and Google, however, it's interesting to note that during the keynote speech in January 2010 when Steve Jobs (Apple's CEO) unveiled the iPad he specifically stated that netbooks are "not better than laptops at anything, they're just cheaper" – a merciless swipe at a product category on which Google are pinning much of their current focus.

Will the iPad replace my Mac or PC at home?

Good question. The short answer is "no". Even if it fulfils all your domestic needs (email, web browsing, eBook reading, say), you will still need to connect it to a Mac or PC so that it can synchronize with iTunes (see below) via a USB connection (the iPad can't sync with iTunes wirelessly). This USB cable, either connected directly to the iPad or to an iPad dock, is how the majority of media content finds its way onto the iPad.

Though you are required to connect to iTunes the first time you use the iPad (to get the device set up), you might then decide to only connect again very infrequently, or whenever you encounter a problem. So in theory, you only really need *access* to a computer.

The advantages of connecting frequently are many, however: not only will you automatically back up your iPad's media and settings, but you will also be prompted to install important software updates from Apple and sync across any photos, videos, music, TV shows, contacts, calendars, bookmarks, etc, that you may have accumulated on your Mac or PC since you last connected. The same goes for media accumulated on the iPad that you might want to sync back into iTunes.

So I definitely need iTunes… umm, what's iTunes?

iTunes is a piece of software produced by Apple for Macs and PCs. It serves three main functions:

• **Media manager** iTunes is used for managing and playing music, video, podcasts and other media on a Mac or PC. This includes everything from importing CDs and making playlists to streaming audio and video to TVs and hi-fi systems around your home.

• **Device manager** iTunes is the program that is used for copying music, movies, photos and other data from a computer to several different Apple devices, including the iPad, iPhone, iPod and the Apple TV.

• **Download store** The iTunes Store (pictured here within the iTunes desktop application) is Apple's legal, pay-to-use music, video and application download service. It's built into iTunes as well as into the iPad itself.

Though many iTunes features are touched on in this book, for the full story, check out *The Rough Guide to iPods & iTunes*.

Can the iPad download music and video directly from the iTunes Store?

Yes, absolutely, though you will need to be connected to a Wi-Fi or cellular data network to get online and access the store. Once the files have downloaded you can watch or listen straight away, and next time you connect your iPad to iTunes on your Mac or PC, the new files are synced back to your iTunes library.

Is my current computer up to the job?

If you bought a PC or Mac in the last few years, it will probably be capable of working with an iPad, but it's certainly worth checking before spending any money. To see the latest on compatible system requirements, visit: apple.com/ipad/specs.

As far as the operating system is concerned, you must have either a Mac running Mac OS X 10.5.8 or later (if you are still using Tiger, it's time to upgrade), or a Windows PC running Windows XP (SP3), Vista or Windows 7. You will also need iTunes 9.0, or later, installed on your Mac or PC.

How does the iPad compare to a Mac or PC for web browsing and email?

Though few pocket-sized Internet devices can match a computer with large screen, mouse and a full-sized keyboard, the iPad does an excellent job of providing the functionality and speed of a full-sized machine, but with the intuitive touch-screen interface of the iPhone. Web browsing is especially well handled, with a great interface for zooming in and out on sections of a webpage and a really handy thumbnail view for moving between pages.

The email tool is impressive too, making excellent use of the real estate on offer in both landscape and portrait modes – the split-column view of the application in landscape mode being particularly pleasing to use.

Can't it edit Word and Excel docs?

The iPad can open, read and forward Word, Excel and PowerPoint docs sent by email or found online. However, to actually edit them you will need to download a third-party application – search the App Store to see what's currently available for the specific document you want to deal with. Also, check out Apple's iWork suite, which includes the **Pages** app (which can edit Word docs) and the **Numbers** app (which can work with Excel docs).

Is the onscreen keyboard easy to use?

Apple are very proud of their touch-screen keyboard and the accompanying error-correcting software that aims to minimize typos. Though typing onto a sheet of glass without the tactile sensation of buttons at your fingertips is at first odd, to say the least, in general, reviewers and owners alike (of both iPads and iPhones) have been pleasantly surprised at how quickly they've got used to it. Inevitably, however, it's not to everyone's taste.

Can I use an iPad as a hard drive to move files between computers?

No, not at present. Unlike the iPod, the iPad doesn't offer a "disk mode" to allow storage of any types of computer files. However, there are many third-party apps (such as **Air Sharing HD** and **iFile**) that allow you to sync files between a computer and an iPad via Wi-Fi.

There are also many apps (including those within the **iWork** suite) that allow you to move files on and off the iPad via the Apps panel (pictured below) within iTunes when an iPad is connected.

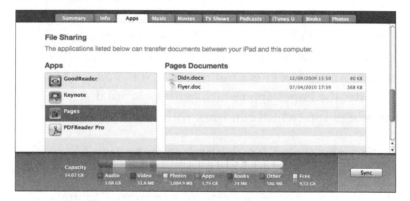

To be honest, given that the iPad isn't the most capacious device ever created, you might be better off buying an inexpensive flash drive or external hard drive to solve your storage needs. Even better, sign up with a service such as SugarSync (sugarsync.com) or Dropbox (dropbox.com) and take your storage and syncing online.

Can I use the iPad as a touch-sensitive control pad for my Mac or PC?

As is so often the case within the world of both iPhones and iPads, "there's an app for that". Though Apple don't include that kind of functionality straight out of the box, there are numerous applications in the App Store that will let you use the iPad in the same way you might the touch-pad on a laptop. **Air Mouse** and **TouchPad** are both worth a look, though the bigger challenge might be trying to keep the iPad still and stable whilst lying on its back on your desk. A few lumps of Blu-Tack work a treat.

Does the IPad feature handwriting recognition technologies?

No, not straight out of the box. But there are several noting apps in the App Store that can handle handwriting recognition… or more likely, fingerwriting recognition. A good example worth looking at is **WritePad**.

eBooks and iBooks

Isn't "iBook" the name of an Apple laptop?

You're not wrong. The iBook was an Apple laptop, produced under various guises between 1999 and 2006, when it disappeared to be superseded by the MacBook. Whether the shift in naming conventions had anything to do with a long-term roadmap that included the

Herman Melville

Moby Dick, or, The Whale

"So be cheery, my lads,
let your hearts never fail,
While   the   bold
harpooneer is striking the
whale!" —NANTUCKET
SONG.

"Oh, the rare old Whale, mid
storm and gale
In his ocean home will be
A giant in might, where
might is right,
And King of the boundless
sea."
—WHALE SONG.

CHAPTER 1.
Loomings.

Call me Ishmael. Som
—never mind how lo
having little or n
purse, and not
interest me o
would sail
watery pa

n in
other,
elings

ar city of
round by
s by coral
nds it with
ft, the streets
. Its extreme
tery, where that

p.
. If

84 of 2461

2461

development of an eBook store is unknown, but the term
is back, and now refers to iBooks, the iPad's eBook reader
app, which also acts as a doorway to Apple's iBookstore.
The store features content from several major publishers,
including HarperCollins and Penguin, as well as a vast
library of free-to-read out-of-copyright classic titles
courtesy of Project Gutenberg. The iBookstore makes its
titles available in the popular ePub eBook format, which
is great for flowing text (say in a novel, pictured), but not
ideal for more picture-heavy, magazine-style publishing
(for these kinds of publication, look to the App Store).

As well as being able to handle ePub titles downloaded
from the iBookstore, the iBooks app can also display titles

from other stores, assuming they peddle their books as DRM-free ePubs. For more on all this, turn to p.106.

What's DRM?

DRM (digital rights management) is the practice of embedding special code in audio, video or eBook files to limit what the user can do with those files. For example, ePub titles downloaded from the iBookstore will only be readable within the iBooks app.

I've bought several Kindle eBooks from Amazon... can I read them on my iPad?

Yes, you can, but not using Apple's homegrown iBooks app; instead you will need to download Amazon's free **Kindle** app from the iTunes App Store. The app syncs seamlessly

with Amazon so that all your Kindle titles are available to read on the iPad.

Aside from the **iBooks** and **Kindle** apps, there are also a whole bunch of other "reader" apps including **Stanza**, **Classics** and **Eucalyptus**. For more on iBooks alternatives, turn to p.114.

Can I read PDF documents on the iPad?

Yes, but again, not using the iBooks application. Instead, PDFs can be viewed on the iPad in much the same way that they can on the iPhone and iPod Touch: i.e., they can be opened via weblinks from Safari, from Mail when sent to the iPad as an email attachment, or through other apps (such as **GoodReader** and **PDF Reader Pro**), which add both file storage and document reader functionality to the iPad – great for books, magazines and journals that have been made available in PDF format. As for annotating PDFs with comments, highlights, etc, take a look at the **iAnnotate PDF** app. For more on PDF apps, see p.118.

Getting technical

What kind of display does the iPad have?

The iPad's screen is glass, with a so-called "oleophobic" coating, first used by Apple on the iPhone 3GS, which makes it far easier to banish greasy smudges and finger marks compared to the screens on earlier iPhone models. The finish on the screen is glossy, which may not be to some people's taste; overall, however, the LED backlighting of the display is bright enough to outweigh any issues caused by reflections.

The iPad uses a liquid crystal display (or LCD) and more specifically, the in-plane switching (IPS) variety. These are incredibly high-quality screens that allow for a wide angle of view without any significant shift in colour or deterioration of the image.

Is the backlighting hard on the eyes?

As with using any computing device with a colour backlit screen, eye strain can be an issue. However, the potential for eye strain is outweighed by the multi-functional nature of the device, the colour screen and the overall build quality of the iPad, when compared to single-function eBook readers such as the Amazon Kindle (even with their matt, black-and-white, eye-easy, E Ink screens).

As for eye strain, the best advice is to simply be aware of the issue and find your own comfort level of screen brightness and time spent reading. Take regular breaks and allow your eyes to refocus on distant objects. It's all common sense really.

What is the back made from?

The back of the iPad is crafted from a single piece of aluminium, with a satin _____ ____. It is similar in feel to the shells of Apple's "unibody" MacBook Air and MacBook Pro laptops.

Does the iPad contain a hard drive?

No. Like the iPod Nano, Touch and Shuffle, and also the iPhone, the iPad stores its information on so-called flash memory: tiny chips of the kind found in digital-camera memory cards and flash drives. These have a smaller capacity than hard drives, but they're less bulky, less power hungry and less likely to break if the device is dropped.

If I buy a 16GB or 32GB model, can I add more internal storage later?

No. What you get is what you get.

The Apple A4 chip

Having previously always purchased their microchips from third-party manufacturers, a couple of years back, Apple took the rather bold step of shelling out $300 million for a California-based computer processor development company called PA Semi so that they could design and manufacture their own. Without going into too many of the techie details, the end result of this acquisition was the in-house development of the "Apple A4" chip and its so-called "system on a chip" (or SOC) design. This 1GHz processor is the one that has ended up under the hood of the first-generation iPads.

The SOC design integrates the main processor with the graphics processor, the memory controller and some other gubbins that would normally exist outside of the processor unit. The end result is allegedly very fast, energy efficient (leading to a longer battery life) and, according to many commentators, likely cheaper to build than doing it the old-fashioned way.

Does it have built-in stereo speakers?

No, the iPad has only the one speaker, which is mono, situated on its lower edge near the Dock connector (though you might be forgiven for thinking there were three speakers due to the way the unibody shell has three speaker vents). It's also worth mentioning that this speaker is surprisingly loud and sounds really pretty good.

The headphone jack, which is located on the iPad's top edge is, however, stereo, and can be used to connect the iPad to an external speaker system. Equally, the Apple iPad Dock (see p.242) features a dedicated stereo line-out socket for connecting to external speaker systems.

Battery questions

Does it take AAs?

No... the iPad comes with an integrated, inaccessible, rechargeable lithium ion battery, which, according to Apple will give you "up to 10 hours" of surfing the web over a Wi-Fi connection, movie playback, or listening to audio content. The battery is recharged via the Dock connector port on the iPad's lower edge when connected using a USB cable to either a computer (Mac or PC) or an Apple power adapter (one of these is included in the box with the iPad), It can also be charged .... of these sources via an Apple iPad Dock.

So what do I do if the battery dies? Can I replace it?

Like those of iPods and iPhones, the iPad's battery gradually dies over time and can only be replaced by Apple for a substantial fee (in the US, the cost is $105.95 including shipping). This lack of user access to the battery is a state of affairs for which Apple have had quite a bit of bad publicity over the years.

To be fair, however, all rechargeable batteries deteriorate over time and eventually die. The high cost of the Apple replacement process can partly be explained by the nature of the device. The power requirements of an iPad are comparable to that of a laptop – and laptop batteries are even more expensive. As for sending the device back to Apple, this is irritating, though at least it means that the device can be properly sealed and free from the flimsy battery flaps that often get broken on non-Apple devices.

I heard that Apple will actually replace the whole iPad if the battery dies. Is this true?

Yes, this is true. For the money you hand over, you'll actually get a replacement iPad. This new iPad will not contain any of the data or content that was on the device that you sent to Apple, so it is essential that you make a backup (see p.91) of the content before you mail it off. For security reasons, you might also want to wipe all your content before heading to the post office, just in case the device goes astray.

Does the Apple warranty cover battery replacement?

The standard Apple warranty will only cover battery replacement for free if the battery turns out to be defective during the period of the warranty. At the time of writing, however, if you purchase the two-year AppleCare cover, then Apple will replace the battery if its capacity drops below fifty percent of its original capacity. Be sure to check the terms and conditions of the AppleCare policy before you sign up, as these details may differ depending on the territory in which you live.

For more on iPad batteries, looking after them, and replacements, turn to p.92.

Internet questions

Does the iPad offer fast Internet access?

That depends where you are and the kind of iPad you have. If you're within range of a Wi-Fi network, as found in homes, offices, cafés (and across some entire cities), then your Internet access will typically be pretty speedy: not quite as fast as with a top-end Mac or PC, but not a long way off.

If, on the other hand, you're out and about, away from any accessible Wi-Fi networks – walking down the street, say, or sitting on a bus – then you will need an iPad with 3G capabilities to stand a chance of getting connected.

What's MobileMe?

Previously known as .Mac, MobileMe is an Apple subscription service that provides a suite of online tools. Available to Mac and PC users, the service allows you to keep multiple computers, and other Apple devices (including the iPad) in sync with each other. For example, when you add a contact or calendar event on your computer, the new details will be instantly "pushed" to your iPad over the air waves.

MobileMe is available as a sixty-day free trial. After that it'll cost you $99/£69 per year. This buys you a large slice of online storage space – 20 GB at the time of writing – along with tools for using it in various ways, such as:

• **Photo and video sharing** Using iPhoto and iMovie, respectively, you can publish your photos and home movies to the web in seconds. You can also upload photos and videos to MobileMe directly from the iPad.

• **Web hosting** iWeb can be used to publish websites, blogs and photo galleries straight into your MobileMe web space.

• **File transfer** The iDisk allows you to store and transfer any type of file via your MobileMe web space. It can also be used to share files that might be too large to send as attachments. Apple produce a free app for accessing your iDisk from your iPad.

• **Email** An email account accessible online and via a mail program. You'll get an address in the form yourname@me.com.

• **Backing up** The MobileMe iDisk can also be a very useful means of backing up key files on your Mac or PC. It can be set to synchronize between the online "cloud" version of your iDisk and an offline duplicate iDisk on your computer.

• **Sync** It's possible to synchronize your contacts, calendars and bookmarks across multiple Macs, PCs and other Apple devices.

• **Remote Mac Access** With MobileMe's "Back to My Mac" feature, you can browse your home computer's files remotely from any other machine that is set up with your MobileMe Account.

• **Find My iPad** This feature lets you remotely track the location of your iPad (when it's online), and either lock or wipe its contents should you need to.

• **Cloud suite** Via your online homepage (found at me.com), you can log into and access all your published sites and galleries, as well as email, calendars, contacts and Safari bookmarks, all housed within a swish cloud-based portal.

None of this is essential, and there are free alternatives to many of the services – such as email and web space. Equally, it's perfectly possible to do backups without any special tools. Still, MobileMe remains attractive, especially to existing Apple users, due to its sheer ease of use. For more, visit apple.com/mobileme.

In this instance you will be connecting via a mobile phone network. The connection will not be as impressive as that experienced over most Wi-Fi networks, but it will be good enough. (For more on the various flavours of cell network connection, see the box on p.21.)

Believe it or not, another factor worth knowing about when out and about is your own speed of travel. If you are travelling on a train or in a moving car, you might find that your connection speed becomes slower than when you are stationary. This is because the device is having to accommodate a constantly shifting relationship to the nearby signal masts that it's connecting with, making it hard for the iPad to maintain a constant and coherent stream of data to and from the Internet.

Will all websites work on an iPad?

The iPad features a fully fledged web browser – Safari – which will work with the overwhelming majority of websites. The main catch is that, at the time of writing, the iPad can't handle Adobe Flash, a web technology used for online animations, video playback, many online games and, in some cases, entire sites.

What's Safari?

Safari is the web browser built into the iPad. It's a streamlined version of the browser shipped on all Macs, and a similar version can also be found on both iPhones and the iPod Touch. Apple also have a PC version available.

Does the iPad synchronize bookmarks with my computer?

Yes. It works with Safari on Macs, and Safari or Internet Explorer on PCs. Firefox isn't currently supported, though the excellent, and free, Xmarks service can be used to unify bookmarks between all your computer browsers. Find out more from xmarks.com.

Will the iPad work with my email account?

For a personal email account, almost certainly. The iPad is compatible with all standard email technologies, such as POP3 and IMAP, and ships preset to work with AOL, Yahoo!, Microsoft Exchange, MobileMe and Gmail (aka Google Mail). If you use Outlook on a PC or Mail on a Mac, the iPad will even sync your account details across from your desktop machine, so you don't have to set anything up.

The only time you're likely to encounter problems is when setting up a work email account. This may or may not be possible, depending on the policies of your network administrators. The only way to be sure is to ask. For more on setting up and using email, turn to p.158.

Does the iPad present any security risks?

Hardly. There's a theoretical risk with any device capable of connecting to Wi-Fi networks that someone could "hack" it remotely and access any stored information. But the risk is extremely small. The only real risk – as with any phone or laptop – is that someone could steal it and access private data. If you're worried about that possibility, the best defence is to password-protect your iPad's screen – look within **Settings > General > Passcode Lock**.

Should I let my children use it to get online?

The iPad doesn't pose any significantly different risks compared to other types of computer that your children might get online with, and there are measures that you can take to make sure that your children stay safe. Under **Settings > General > Restrictions**, set access options for iTunes content and also determine whether others can download some kinds of content at all. You can also block access to YouTube and Safari completely if you wish.

Because, at the time of writing, the iPad does not support different user accounts for different members of the family, all these settings can be a bit of a hassle, so also talk to your kids about online safety so that they can develop their own online security skills.

Oh, and while I think of it...

Will the iPad work with my old iPhone and iPod accessories?

Maybe. The Dock socket on the bottom of the iPad is the same as those on recent iPods and iPhones, so accessories that connect via this socket should be able to connect. That doesn't necessarily mean they'll work, however. At the time of writing, the success rate seems to be around fifty-fifty, as many older devices don't support the newer operating system that runs on the iPad.

Does it have Voice Command, like recent iPhone models do?

No, unfortunately it doesn't.

Is the iPad good for games?

Yes, absolutely. In the same way that games took off at an unprecedented rate on the iPhone, developers have moved quickly to show what's possible on the device, and there's an ever expanding category within the App Store dedicated to gaming apps. Add to that the launch of Games Center (Apple's online social gaming network, which will be made available for the iPad via the OS 4 software update in late 2010) and you have a pretty compelling gaming platform.

For reviews of all the newest and coolest games, visit slidetoplay.com, toucharcade.com or eurogamer.net/iphone.

Okay, I'm sold on the idea; where can I get one?

Read on, and all will be revealed

Buying options

Which model? Where from?

At the time of going to press there are only two hardware decisions you really need to make: how much storage space you need your iPad to have, and what sort of connectivity you want to go for (Wi-Fi or Wi-Fi+3G). In this chapter we'll take a look at these two questions and also touch upon various other buying options you might want to think about.

How many gigs do you need?

Choosing between the various iPad models is partly a matter of choosing how much storage capacity to go for. Remember that you don't necessarily need an iPad capable of holding your entire music or video collection. You can store your whole collection on your computer's hard drive and just copy across to your iPad the songs or albums you want to listen to at any one time. The same goes for your photo collection – you don't need to keep it all on both your iPad and regular computer.

Checking your current data needs

If you already use iTunes to store music and video, then you can easily get an idea of how much space your existing collection takes up. On the left, click **Music**, **Movies**, **Podcasts** or any playlist and the bottom of the iTunes window will reveal the total disk space that the selected item occupies (as pictured below).

As for photographs, the size of the images on your computer and the amount of space they occupy there bears little relation to the space the same images will take up on an iPad. This is because when iTunes copies photos to your iPad, it resizes them for use on the device. As a rough guide, three thousand images will take up around 1GB on your iPad.

What are the options?

At the time of writing, there are three storage sizes available: 16GB, 32GB and 64GB. In terms of actual available capacity for music, apps and the like, assume that around 1GB of your iPad's space is taken up by the operating system and the rest is available for use.

Interestingly, during the run-up to the US launch of the iPad, pre-orders through the Apple website favoured the lowest-capacity device by almost two-to-one over the highest-capacity version, perhaps suggesting that either early adopters were not looking to invest too much money on the first version of the model, or that they genuinely saw its use as primarily a web browsing or email device, and not somewhere to store loads of content. This idea is certainly worth thinking about, as you really might not need as much capacity as you think, especially if you primarily intend to use the iPad at home.

> **Tip:** For the latest iPad tech specs and prices, visit the Apple website: apple.com/ipad.

Wi-Fi or Wi-Fi+3G?

As already mentioned, there is also the connectivity question to be addressed. If you only intend to use the iPad at home, and have a wireless network up and running, then go for the Wi-Fi-only model; if you intend to take the thing

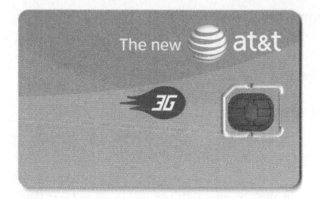

out and about, then there is a strong case for going for the
Wi-Fi+3G version. In the latter case, you are going to need
a SIM card and to sign up for a 3G service plan (see p.85).
In many countries, you can buy a Micro SIM card from
the Apple Store when you buy your iPad; if not, you'll have
to get one direct from a network provider. The Apple site
is the best place to compare the available tariffs and deals.
Visit apple.com/ipad/3g and click on the flag, bottom right,
to find your country's page.

The nature of the service plans varies slightly from
territory to territory, though all have roughly the same
setup. In the US, for example, there are two options
available through AT&T: $15 a month for 250MB of data,
or unlimited data for $29.99 a month. Both can be prepaid
a month in advance, and there is no lengthy contract,
which means that you might only pay it up every now
and again, and for only a month at a time, perhaps when
heading out of town on a trip.

But you don't have to go with any particular cellular provider – any data network provider will do, as long as they can supply you with a Micro SIM card compatible with the iPad SIM tray.

What about data roaming?

Your domestic data plan is unlikely to include data roaming (using 3G to access the web, send emails, etc, when abroad). It's worth checking what local plans are available in the country you're intending to visit (look on their local Apple website) as the cheapest option is likely to be buying a pre-paid Micro SIM to put into your iPad when you reach your destination. There are also third parties offering Micro SIM roaming packs. If you're travelling to Europe, check out maxroam.com.

Where to buy

As with all Apple products, iPads cost basically the same amount no matter where you buy them. The price you'll get direct from Apple...

- **Apple Store UK** apple.com/ukstore

- **Apple Store US** apple.com/store

...will typically be only a few pounds/dollars more (or occasionally less) than the price you'll find from the many other dealers that sell online or on the high street. That said, different sellers may throw in different extras, such as

a case or dock, to get your attention. In the US market you can keep track of these various offers and discounts at the brilliant "Buyers' Guides" section of:

- **Mac Review Zone** macreviewzone.com

Or try a price-comparison agent such as, in the US:

- **Google Product Search** google.com/products

- **PriceWatch** pricewatch.com

- **Shopper.com** shopper.com

- **Shopping.com** shopping.com

In the UK, price-comparison agents include:

- **Kelkoo** kelkoo.co.uk

- **Shopping.com** uk.shopping.com

Buying from a high-street store typically means paying the full standard price, but you'll get the iPad immediately.

If you order over the phone or Internet from Apple, you can expect up to a week's wait for delivery. For a list of dealers in the UK, follow the link from apple.com/uk/hardware.

In many US and UK cities, you can also go straight to one of Apple's own high-street stores, such as the iconic New York City Fifth Avenue branch, pictured here. For a list of all the stores, see:

- **Apple Stores** apple.com/retail

However, some online retailers tend to be quite quick to deliver, including the best-known of all:

- **Amazon US** amazon.com

- **Amazon UK** amazon.co.uk

Warranties and insurance

If you buy through either the Apple online store or in a bricks-and-mortar Apple Store, then expect to get offered the AppleCare Protection Plan. For $99 (US) you will get two years of cover from the date of purchase instead of the standard one year that you get for free. This covers defects and failures that have not been caused by "damage or abuse". It also covers the replacement of the iPad if its battery capacity drops to less than fifty percent of the iPad's original capacity. This price will also give you unlimited telephone technical support for the period of the warranty. Double-check the terms and conditions in your territory, as they might be different to those described above.

It might also be worth investigating the possibility of adding the iPad to your existing home contents insurance, as this sometimes even includes certain items when taken with you outside of the home. Equally, some insurers also offer special insurance packages for high-value electronic devices.

Used iPads

Refurbished iPads

Though at the time of writing it is a little early in the product's life for this to kick in, Apple, and a few retailers, will offer refurbished iPads. These will either be end-of-line models or up-to-date ones that have been returned for some reason. They come "as new" – checked, repackaged and with a full standard warranty – but they are reduced in price by up to forty percent (usually more like fifteen percent). The only problem is availability: the products are in such hot demand that you need to check in regularly to see the real bargains, and when you do spot something you want, you shouldn't expect much time to mull over the purchase, as it will probably go to someone else if you decide to sleep on it.

In both the UK and US sites, follow the Special Deals links from apple.com/ukstore and apple.com/store respectively; and in the US, for the most up-to-date information about availability, call 1-800/MY-APPLE. Alternatively, check with your local Apple retailer to see whether they offer refurbished or returned iPads.

Secondhand iPads

Buying a secondhand iPad is much like buying any other piece of used electronic equipment: you might find a bargain but you might land yourself with an overpriced table mat. If you buy one that is less than a year old (and any offered secondhand before April 2011 will be), it will still be within warranty, so you should be able to get it repaired for free if anything goes wrong inside – even if the iPad in question was purchased in a different country.

Whatever you buy, it's good to see it in action before parting with any cash, but remember that this won't tell

you everything. If an iPad's been used a lot, for example, the battery might be on its last legs and soon need replacing, which will add substantially to the cost.

If possible, see if you can negotiate a couple of days with the device before you hand over the cash... that way you can see how well it holds its charge during use.

If you buy on eBay (the excellent **eBay** app is pictured here), you'll get loads of choice and a certain level of protection against getting sold a dud. But be sure to read the auction listing carefully and ask the seller questions if you're unsure of anything.

To buy or to wait?

When shopping for any piece of computer equipment, there's always the tricky question of whether to buy the current model, which may have been around for a few months, or hang on for the next version, which may be better *and* less expensive. In the case of iPads, the situation is worse than normal, because Apple are famously secretive about their plans to release new or upgraded versions of their hardware.

Unless you have a friend who works in Apple HQ – and an opportunity to get them drunk – you're unlikely to hear anything from the horse's mouth about new iPad models until the day they appear. So, unless a new model came out recently, there's always the possibility that your new purchase will be out of date within a few weeks. About the best you can do is check out some sites where rumours of new models are discussed. But don't believe everything you read…

- **Apple Insider** appleinsider.com

- **Mac Rumors** macrumors.com

Setting up

Syncing and finding your way around

Setting up a new iPad is usually a simple process. With a little luck, and assuming that your computer is up to the job, it shouldn't take you much more than an hour to get everything up and running and copy across some music, videos, photos, contacts and calendars from your Mac or PC. However, you may first need to grab the latest version of iTunes...

Download the latest iTunes

If you've ever used an iPod or iPhone, you'll already be familiar with iTunes – Apple's application for managing music, videos, apps, photos, podcasts and more. As with the iPod and iPhone, iTunes is the bridge between your iPad and your computer.

Even if you already use iTunes, you may need to update to the latest version to get it to work with the iPad. New versions come out every month or so, and it's always worth having the latest. To make sure you have the most recent version, open iTunes and, on a Mac, choose **Check for Updates...** from the **iTunes** menu and, on a PC, look for the same option, but in the **Help** menu.

If you don't already use iTunes...

All recent Macs have iTunes pre-installed – you'll find it in the **Applications** folder and on the Dock. Open it up and check for updates, as described above. If you have a PC, however, you'll need to download iTunes from Apple:

• **iTunes** apple.com/itunes

Once you've downloaded the installer file, double-click it and follow the prompts. Either during the installation or the first time you run iTunes, you'll be presented with a few options. Don't worry too much about these as you'll be able to change them later within iTunes **Preferences**.

Cables and charging

The iPad comes with a USB charge/sync cable. One end attaches to the iPad (either directly or via a Dock), the other end connects to any USB port – on a Mac, PC, on the supplied power adapter, on a USB hub, etc. If you have a USB cable from a recent iPod or iPhone, this should also work with your iPad.

To charge your iPad, simply connect it to a USB port – either on a computer or a USB power adapter. Note, however, that if you're charging via a computer, the USB port in question will need to be "powered". The vast majority of USB sockets meet this criterion, but some, especially those on keyboards and other peripherals, may not work. Also note that your iPad usually won't charge from a Mac or PC in sleep or standby mode.

When the iPad is charging, the battery icon at the top-right of the screen will display a lightning slash. When it's fully charged this will change to a plug.

If your iPad's power becomes so low that the device can't function, you may well find that plugging it in to charge will not revive it straight away. Don't worry – it should come back to life after ten minutes or so.

If you're in a hurry to charge, don't use or sync the iPad while it's charging – this will slow down the process. You can cancel the sync with the slider on the iPad's screen – or by "ejecting" the iPad from iTunes via the icon in the iTunes sidebar. For more on your iPad battery's life, see p.92.

Connecting for the first time

The first time it's turned on, the iPad will ask you to connect to iTunes. Do this using the supplied USB cable; it makes no difference whether you connect to a Mac or PC, just that iTunes is present. Though the iPad doesn't have an official "activation" process (like the iPhone does), you do need to make this iTunes connection to get things started, even if you have no intention of syncing across any data.

Disconnecting an iPad

All the iPad's functions remain available when it is connected to iTunes, though if you start tapping on the screen while the device is syncing, the sync will be interrupted. Likewise, the iPad can be disconnected at any time, even halfway through a sync. Despite this, iTunes still offers an eject button (⏏) next to the iPad's icon. This allows you to remove the iPad from iTunes (it no longer appears in the sidebar) but leave it charging.

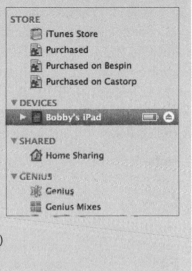

As part of the process you'll need to enter your iTunes Account details (Apple ID or MobileMe details will also work), even if you don't want to download content from the iTunes Store, Apps Store or iBookstore. If you don't have an account, you'll need to set one up, specifying a valid credit card billing address and payment details... it's these details that determine which of the various country-specific download stores you'll have access to.

If you have an ... ... ith Wi-Fi and 3G, you may well also be prompted to sign up for a data plan. ... ... on this take a look at the Connecting chapter of this book.

Synchronizing

Once your iPad and iTunes have made acquaintance, you'll find yourself presented with the various tabs (pictured here) that control how the iPad is synchronized with your computer. Take a look at the options within each tab and make selections by checking the various boxes on offer. Many of the specifics are covered in more detail elsewhere in this book, but to get you started...

> • **Info** Lets you synchronize contacts, mail accounts, calendars, notes and bookmarks from your computer. Once set up, changes or additions made on the computer will be reflected on your iPad, and vice versa.

> **Tip:** MobileMe, Google and Exchange users can set up their server-based syncs directly on the iPad (see p.183).

• **Audio and video** There are various tabs for automatically syncing audio and video content to the iPad. If you'd rather simply drag and drop music and video onto your iPad, click **Summary > Manually manage music and videos**. Note that media downloaded directly onto the iPad, or playlists created on the iPad, are copied back to iTunes when you sync.

• **Photos** iTunes moves photos from your selected application or folder and gives you the option, each time you connect, to import back to your computer images that have been added to the iPad's Saved Photos album since you last synced.

> **Tip:** To stop iPhoto on a Mac opening when your iPad connects, open **Applications > Image Capture**, and then look for the option under **Image Capture > Preferences**.

Forcing a sync

When you choose from any of the above options, click **Apply** to start syncing straight away. You can also initiate a sync at any time by clicking **Sync** in iTunes (bottom-right) or by right-clicking your iPad's icon in the iTunes sidebar and choosing the option from there.

Seeing what's on your iPad

At any time while connected, you can click the triangle to the left of your iPad's iTunes icon to see the music, video and Podcasts that it's currently storing.

> **Tip:** To change your iPad's name, tap on the label next to its icon in iTunes and type in whatever you want.

Syncing with multiple computers

When you connect your iPad to a different computer, it will appear in iTunes (as long as it's a recent version of iTunes) with all the sync options unchecked. You can then skip through the various tabs and choose to overwrite some or all of the current content…

• **Music, video and podcasts** Adding music, video or podcasts from a second computer will erase all of the existing media from the iPad. This applies even if you have "Manually manage music and videos" turned on. Next time you connect at home, you can reload your own media, but you won't be able to copy the new material back onto your computer.

> **Tip:** You can purchase via multiple iTunes Accounts on an iPad, but only sync those purchases to iTunes if your computer is "authorized" for the accounts (see p.99).

• **Photos** Can be synced from a new machine without affecting music, video, apps or any other content. However, to leave everything other than photos intact, you need to hit **Cancel** when iTunes offers to synchronize the "Account Information".

• **Apps** You can add apps from a second machine (even if it uses a different iTunes Account) without overwriting existing apps on the iPad; however, you won't be able to sync all the new apps back to your machine at home without "authorizing" it for the other iTunes Account (see p.99).

• **Info** When you add contacts, calendars, email accounts or bookmarks from a second computer, you have two choices – either merging the new and existing data, or simply overwriting the existing data.

Getting to know your iPad

Settings and basic functions

Once your iPad is stocked up with all your media and data, you're ready to acquaint yourself with some of the basic settings controls, add a few personal customizations and generally make it your own...

Wallpaper

Tap **Settings > Brightness & Wallpaper** to choose the photo that appears on either your Lock Screen, your Home Screen, or both. Apple have a few ideas preloaded, but you can also choose from your own photos and drag and crop the photo before setting it. When choosing a picture for your Home Screen, try and keep things minimal, as it can get pretty hard to deal with all your app icons over a busy image.

Tip: If you want a solid colour background, you'll need to roll your own using a painting app such as **Brushes**.

Auto-Lock

Within **Settings > General**, you can set the number of minutes of inactivity before your iPad goes to sleep and locks its screen. In order to maximize battery life, leave it set to one minute unless you find this setting too annoying.

Sounds

Within **Settings > General > Sounds**, various sounds can be disabled. Keyboard clicks are the most likely contender for deactivation... even if they don't bother you, be sure that they annoy everyone around you.

> **Tip:** To quickly mute the iPad's sound, press and hold the volume-down button on the device's edge.

Privacy

As already mentioned, if you want to protect the private data on your iPad – and make sure no one ever uses it without your consent – apply a passcode. Tap **Settings > General > Passcode Lock**, and choose a four-digit number. If you later forget the code, connect your iPad to your computer and restore it from the iPad **Summary** tab. If a thief tries this, they'll get the iPad working, but by that stage all your private data will have been wiped.

Parental controls

The iPad also features parental controls (found within **Settings > General > Restrictions**) and you'll find a host of ways to make the iPad child-friendly – blocking access to YouTube, for example, or to songs tagged as "explicit".

The Home Screen

The Home Screen is the launch pad for the iPad's various applications. The iPad can support multiple Home Screens, which can be a useful way of separating out your apps by category (by late 2010, the grouping of apps will also be made possible by the Folders feature of iPhone OS 4).

To move between the various screens, simply swipe your finger left or right. Note that just above the Dock on each Home Screen is a row of dots that represents the number of Home Screens you have created, with the currently active screen highlighted.

Tip: You can also move between screens by tapping to either side of these Home Screen dots.

Customizing the layout

To rearrange the icons on the Home Screen, simply touch any icon for a few seconds until all the icons start to wobble. You can now press and hold any icon to detach it (you will see the icon lift slightly, as if stuck to your

finger) and then drag it into a new position, including onto separate Home Screens (by dragging to either the left or right edge of the screen), or onto the Dock at the bottom of the screen. Up to six icons can live on the Dock; if it is already full, first drag one of the existing six out of the way.

To delete an icon that you added, simply tap its ⊗ icon. Annoyingly, you can't delete Apple's built-in icons, but you can move them to a screen you visit less frequently.

Once everything is laid out how you want it, click the **Home** button to fix all the app icons in place.

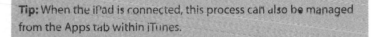

Tip: When the iPad is connected, this process can also be managed from the Apps tab within iTunes.

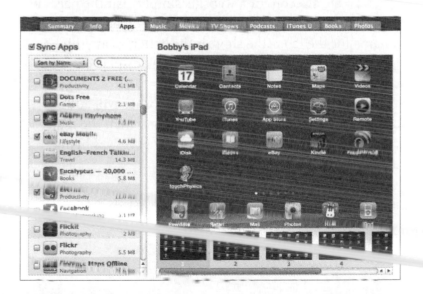

The iPad also allows you to easily move icons onto different Home Screens, which you can switch between with the flick of a finger. This can be useful if you want to move icons you rarely use out of the way or arrange your apps by task or category (say, all your games on one screen, and all your reading and news apps on another).

Adding websites

If you regularly visit a particular website – a newspaper or blog, for example – then add an icon (a "web-clip") for that site on your Home Screen. This way, you don't have to open Safari and tap in an address or search through your bookmarks each time you want to visit the site.

To create an icon for a website, simply visit the page in Safari and press **+**. Select **Add to Home Screen** and choose a name for the icon (the shorter the better, as anything longer than around ten characters won't display completely on the Home Screen).

When you add a web-clip some websites will add a default icon to your Home Screen. If not, then the iPad creates an icon for it based on how the page was being displayed at the time.

> **Tip:** To make the best-looking and most readable icons, try zooming in on the logo of the website in question before tapping the **Add to Home Screen** button.

The Home button

Whatever activity you are doing on the iPad, a single tap of the Home button (the one physical button on the front of the iPad) takes you back into the Home Screens... generally to the Home Screen that you last visited if you have multiple screens running. A second tap takes you to the far-left Home Screen; and a third tap takes you to the Search Screen (see p.72).

The Home button can also be double-tapped to either take you to the far-left Home Screen (by default), the Search Screen, or to display iPod controls when playing music whilst using other apps (arguably the most useful function). To make your choice, look for the options within **Settings > General > Home**.

Searching your iPad

When viewing the farthest Home Screen to the left, the iPad's Search Screen is accessed by either a swipe to the left, or a single tap of the Home button. As already mentioned, you can also set the iPad to take you to the Search Screen when the Home button is double-tapped (**Settings > General > Home**).

Get into the habit of quickly popping to the Search Screen to find emails, calendar events or a friend's contact details. You'll soon find that it's much faster than navigating via specific apps.

To choose exactly what content from your iPad is searched, check and uncheck the options within **Settings > General > Home > Search Results**. Here, you can also change the order in which results are displayed, by dragging the ≡ icons up and down the list.

> **Tip:** If you tap ⌨ to hide the keyboard on the Search Screen, you will find the Dock lurking behind.

Typing and text tips

The iPad's touchscreen keyboard isn't to everyone's taste, but if you can get used to it, the iPad allows for typing far faster than you might expect. Following are some tips to get you started. The best places to practise are in the iPad's Notes application or a draft email in Mail.

Basic techniques

• **Using the keys** The iPad enters a letter or symbol when you release your finger, not when you touch the screen.

• **Popover options** Many keys reveal useful alternative characters in little popover windows when you tap and hold. For example, tap and hold the letter "e" to reveal various versions of the letter with accents… simply slide to the one you want and release your finger. Many symbol and punctuation keys also reveal alternatives when held.

• **Numbers and punctuation** To reveal these keys, tap ?123.

• **Symbols** To reveal these keys, tap ?123 followed by #+=.

• **Edits and navigating** You can tap anywhere in your text to jump to that point. For more accuracy, tap, hold and then slide around to see a magnifying glass containing a cursor.

Tip: In many instances you can banish the keyboard by tapping its ⌨ key.

Speed-typing tips

• **Quick full stops** When you reach the end of a sentence, double-tap the space bar to add a full stop and a space. If this trick doesn't work, turn the relevant option on in **Settings > General > Keyboard**.

• **One-touch punctuation** Tap  and then slide to the relevant key without taking your finger off the screen. Much more convenient than tapping twice.

• **One-touch caps** The same trick works with capital letters: tap **Shift** (⇧) and slide to a letter.

• **Caps Lock** If you like to TYPE IN CAPS, turn on the Caps Lock feature under **Settings > General > Keyboard**. You can then double-tap the **Shift** key (⇧) to toggle Caps Lock on and off.

• **Thumbs and fingers** When using the iPad in landscape mode, use your fingers on the keyboard just as you would a regular keyboard. However, for portrait mode, experiment with holding the iPad with both hands so that you can type with two thumbs. It feels like a bit of a stretch at first, but actually works pretty well.

• **One touch at a time** If typing with two thumbs or multiple fingers, only let one finger touch the screen at a time. If the first finger is still on the screen, the second tap won't be recognized.

Tip: To get your onscreen typing up to speed, check out a trainer app such as **TapTyping**.

Auto-correct and prediction

At first, it's tricky to hit every key accurately on the iPad, but usually that doesn't matter much, thanks to the device's ingenious word-prediction software. Even if you hit only half the right letters, the iPad will usually work out what you meant by looking at the keys adjacent to the ones you tapped and comparing each permutation of letters to those in its dictionary of words.

• **Accepting and rejecting suggestions** When the iPad suggests a word or name it will appear in a little bubble under the word you're typing. To accept the suggestion, just keep typing as normal – hit space, return or a punctuation mark. To reject it, tap the suggestion bubble, and then finish typing the word that you want.

• **Dictionary** The iPad has an excellent dictionary, which includes, for example, many names and swear words. In addition, it learns all names stored in your contacts and any word that you've typed twice and rejected the suggested correction. Unfortunately, it's not currently possible to edit the dictionary, but you can blank it and start again. Tap **Settings > General > Reset > Reset Keyboard Dictionary**.

Tip: If you're ever stuck for an obscure spelling or meaning, download the free **Dictionary.com** iPad app.

• **Auto-capitalization** In addition to correcting letters, the iPad will add punctuation (changing "i" to "I'm" for example) and capitalize the first letter of words at the start of sentences. If you prefer to stick with lower case, turn off Auto-capitalization within **Settings > General > Keyboard**.

Cut, Copy and Paste

Among the most useful features on the iPad are the **Cut**, **Copy** and **Paste** commands – especially if you don't particularly get on with the device's keyboard. Though at first they can seem a little fiddly to use, it really is worth getting acquainted with the taps and drags that bring these controls to life. And we are not only talking about text; these options will also pop up for copying images, or even entire webpages.

• **1** Locate the text or word you want to copy or cut and then tap and hold until an options bubble appears; choose **Select** to highlight that word, or **Select All** for the whole piece of prose of which your word is a part.

• **2** Use the blue end-point markers to drag the size of the selection you have highlighted, and then when you are ready, tap **Copy** or **Cut** in the option bubble. Both actions move the selection onto the iPad's "clipboard", ready to be pasted elsewhere.

Tip: If you want a specific app for organizing copied content on a clipboard, try **Pastebot**.

• **3** Navigate to the place where you want to paste the text (which might be a completely different app, an email you are composing, or perhaps the search field in Safari).

• **4** Tap and hold at your desired point and choose **Paste** from the option bubble that appears. You can alternatively **Select** text (as above) and then **Paste** over the top of it.

Replace

The option bubble that appears when you select composed text sometimes also offers up the **Replace** command. This has nothing to do with replacing text with the contents of the clipboard – that's what **Paste** is for – but is instead used to find common alternatives to words that you may have mistyped. It's not one hundred percent accurate (as pictured below), but can still be a useful alternative to retyping the whole word.

Mary had a little lamp, its fleece was white as snow

Wake/Sleep and On/Off

On the top edge of the iPad (when held in portrait mode) can be found the Sleep/Wake button. Just like its counterpart on iPhones and iPod Touch, this button can be pressed to put the iPad into Sleep mode (the screen darkens). A second press and the iPad wakes up to reveal the Lock Screen (pictured here).

If you press and hold the button for a few seconds you are prompted to "Slide and power off", which completely shuts down the iPad. Press and hold the button again until you see an Apple logo to turn the iPad back on.

Tip: Power the iPad on and off at least once a week to clear caches and you'll find that it runs much more smoothly.

Picture Frame mode

Working much like a traditional screensaver, the iPad's Picture Frame mode displays a cycle of your photos on the iPad's screen. To kick things off, tap the flower icon to the right of the "slide to unlock" control on the Lock Screen.

Once running, tapping either the screen or Home button reveals the Lock Screen controls; tapping the flower icon can then be used to turn Picture Frame mode off and return you to your regular Lock Screen.

Various options can be found for this feature within **Settings > Picture Frame**. The Origami setting is good fun, and you also get to choose whether you want to use all your photos or only a specific album.

Rotation Lock

The iPad, like the iPhone and iPod Touch, features a rotation sensor that turns the screen to keep its content upright as you rotate the device between portrait and landscape positions.

> **Tip:** Get used to finding the iPad's hardware switches, whichever bevel the Home button's on.

At any time you can lock the screen orientation using the Rotation Lock switch found above the volume controls – particularly useful when reading in bed.

Accessibility tools

The iPad comes loaded with several accessibility tools designed to aid the blind and visually impaired. To see what's available, and play with the options, tap through to **Settings > General > Accessibility**. Features include:

- **VoiceOver** Used to speak items of text on the screen. Touch an item to hear it spoken, double-tap to select it and use three fingers to scroll.

- **Screen zoom** Once set up, double-tapping with three fingers will zoom you in and out of the screen; dragging with three fingers moves you around the screen.

> **Tip:** Interestingly, **Zoom** sometimes does a better job of rendering iPhone apps than the built-in 2x feature.

- **Color inversion** Renders the screen as a negative image, making blacks white, whites black, etc.

For those whose hearing is impaired, an option for turning on closed-captioning for video can be found within **Settings > Video**.

Getting online

Via Wi-Fi, Bluetooth and 3G

The iPad can handle various kinds of wireless signal: all models can deal with Wi-Fi, for Internet access in homes, offices and public hotspots; and Bluetooth, for connecting to compatible headsets and carphone systems. There are also iPad models that support 3G connectivity, for connecting when out and about, and out of reach of Wi-Fi networks. This chapter takes a quick look at each.

Using Wi-Fi

Connecting to networks

To connect to a Wi-Fi network, tap **Settings > Wi-Fi** and choose a network from the list. If it's a secure wireless network (as indicated by the padlock icon), the iPad will invite you to enter the relevant password.

Though this procedure doesn't take long, it's best to have the iPad point you in the direction of Wi-Fi networks automatically. This way, whenever you open an Internet-based tool such as Maps or Mail, and there are no known networks in range, the iPad will present you with a list of all the networks it can find. You can turn this feature on and off via **Settings > Wi-Fi > Ask to Join Networks**.

If the network you want to connect to isn't in the list, you could be out of range, or it could be that it's a "hidden" network, in which case tap **Wi-Fi > Other** and enter its name, password and password type.

> **Tip:** To view the signal strength of a connected Wi-Fi network, look to the 🛜 icon on the iPad's Status Bar.

> **Tip:** If you want to check how fast your connection is over either Wi-Fi or 3G, download the **SpeedtestX HD** app.

Forgetting networks

Once you've connected to a Wi-Fi network, your iPad will remember it as a trusted network and connect to it automatically whenever you're in range. This is useful but can be annoying – if, for example, it keeps connecting to a network you once chose accidentally, or one which lets you connect but doesn't provide web access. In these cases, click on the ⊙ icon next to the relevant network name within **Settings > Wi-Fi** and tap **Forget this Network**. This won't stop you connecting to it manually in the future.

> **Tip:** If you want to maximize battery life, get into the habit of turning Wi-Fi off when you're not using it.

Finding public hotspots

Many cafés, hotels, airports and other public places offer wireless Internet access, though often you'll have to pay for the privilege of using them – particularly in establishments which are part of big chains (Starbucks and the like). You either pay the person running the system (over the counter in a café, for instance) or connect and sign up onscreen. If you use such services a lot, you may save time and money by signing up with a service such as Boingo or T-Mobile, which allow you to connect at thousands of hotspots for a monthly fee.

- **Boingo** boingo.com

- **T-Mobile** t-mobile.com/hotspot

If you have a 3G iPad, you might also find that your data plan entitles you to use thousands of Wi-Fi hotspots as well as the 3G network… check with your provider to see what they offer.

The ideal, of course, is to stick to free hotspots. There are various online directories that will help you locate them, though none is comprehensive:

- **WiFinder** wifinder.com

- **ZONE Finder** wi-fi.jiwire.com

It's worth knowing that you can also search for hotspots nearby using the **Google Maps** app – simply load the map for the area you are interested in and then type "wifi" into the search field (of course, you will need an Internet connection to do this, so plan on s…… for some likely hotspots before you head out the door).

When it won't connect...

If your iPad refuses to connect to a Wi-Fi network, try again, in case you mistyped the password or tapped the wrong network name. If you still have no luck, try the following:

• **Try WEP Hex** If there's a ⊙ icon in the password box, tap it, choose **WEP Hex** and try again.

• **Check the settings** Some networks, especially in offices, require you to manually enter information such as an IP address. Ask your network administrator for the details and plug them in by clicking ⊙ next to the relevant network name.

• **Add your MAC address** Some routers in homes and offices (but not in public hotspots) will only allow access to devices specified in the router's "access list". If this is the case, you'll need to enter the iPad's MAC address – which you'll find within **Settings > General > About > Wi-Fi Address** – to your router's list. This usually means entering the router's setup screen and looking for something titled **MAC Filtering** or **Access List**.

• **Reboot the router** If you're at home, try rebooting your wireless router by turning it off or unplugging it for a few seconds. Turn off the Wi-Fi on the iPad (**Settings > Wi-Fi**) until the router has rebooted.

• **Tweak your router settings** If the above doesn't work, try temporarily turning off your router's wireless password to see whether that fixes the problem. If it does, try choosing a different type of password (WEP rather than WPA, for example). If that doesn't help, you could try updating the firmware (internal software) of the router, in case the current version isn't compatible with the iPad's hardware. Check the manufacturer's website to see if a firmware update is available.

3G, GPRS and EDGE

In your home country, assuming you're in an area with network coverage, and assuming you have a data plan set up, a 3G-capable iPad should automatically connect to your carrier's data network. When your iPad connects to the Internet using the cellular data network, one of three icons will appear in the Status Bar: **3G** (which is fastest), **E** (for EDGE), or ° (for GPRS, which is slowest). Cellular data networks will automatically give way to Wi-Fi (which is usually faster) whenever possible.

Setting up data plans

Setting up a 3G data plan on the iPad is very easy, though the specifics of each carrier's plan may differ between territories. To get started, insert the Micro SIM supplied by your network provider, then tap **Settings > Cellular Data**. Tap **Cellular Data Plan** and follow the onscreen instructions.

The iPad is unlocked, so you can go with whoever you like, assuming they can provide an appropriate data plan and a Micro SIM card (smaller than a regular SIM card). Check apple.com for providers offering suitable plans.

Data usage and quotas

Depending on the territory in which you live, you may well sign up for a data plan that gives you a set amount of data usage each month (in the US for example, AT&T

offer both 250MB and unlimited monthly plans). The iPad will monitor your usage and warn you as you run out – at twenty percent, ten percent and zero remaining. When you go over your limit, either top up, or move onto the unlimited option.

> **Tip:** Consider switching from power-hungry 3G to EDGE (**Settings > Cellular Data**) when your battery is low.

You can check to see how much of your data plan quota is left at any time by tapping **Settings > Cellular Data > View Account**.

Connecting abroad

When overseas, you can activate international roaming within **Settings > Cellular Data**, but be aware that you may well get charged hefty roaming charges for the privilege if you use the same data plan you use at home. It's worth checking with your carrier to see what the situation is with partner carriers in the country you intend to travel to. A better alternative is to research the equivalent data plans in your destination country and pick up an iPad-compatible micro-SIM card when you get there.

As for Internet, Wi-Fi should work wherever you are – for free, if you can find a non-charging hotspot.

> **Tip:** 3G-capable iPads also feature a GPS chip, which can locate your position even with data-roaming off.

Airplane mode

Only appearing on 3G-capable iPads, the iPad's **Airplane Mode** is quickly accessible at the top of the **Settings** menu, and lets you temporarily disable GSM, EDGE, 3G, Wi-Fi and Bluetooth, enabling you to use non-wireless features, such as the iPod, during a flight, or in any other circumstances where cellular and wireless signal data use is not permitted. (Whether such signals actually cause any risk on aircraft is disputed, but that's another story.)

Tip: Owners of non-3G iPads should make sure that Wi-Fi is turned off within Settings > WI-Fi before they fly.

Bluetooth

Bluetooth allows computers, phones, printers and other devices to communicate at high speeds over short distances. The iPad's Bluetooth feature can be used to connect the device to certain peripherals, such as Bluetooth keyboards and headphones. Certain third-party apps also use Bluetooth to connect the iPad to the iPhone – the excellent **Camera For iPad**, for example, allows you to utilize the iPhone's camera, via a Bluetooth connection, to take photo... ...ately from the iPad.

You can turn Bluetooth on and off... ...ping **Settings > General > Bluetooth**. If you're not using it, leave it switched off to help maximize battery life.

VPN

A VPN, or Virtual Private Network, allows a private office network to be made available over the Internet. If your office network uses a VPN to allow access to an Intranet, file servers, a Microsoft Exchange Server, or whatever, you'll probably find that your iPad can connect to it.

> **Tip:** With your administrator's help, Exchange servers can also be set up within **Settings > Mail, Contacts, Calendars.**

The iPad supports most VPN systems, so ask your administrator for details and a "configuration profile", which can be used to get things set up. You'll find all the VPN settings on the iPad under **Settings > General > Network > VPN.**

VPN desktop connections

You can also use VPN technology to set up your own dedicated connection back to your home computer from the iPad, allowing you to view the screen, files, applications – the whole shebang – from the iPad when away from home. There are several third-party apps that will make this happen for you; they can be quite techie to set up, but are worth trying out if you feel brave. Search for VPN in the App Store, or try your luck with our recommendation: **iTeleport for iPad**.

Maintenance

Troubleshooting and keeping things ship-shape

The iPad is basically a computer and, just like its full-sized cousins, it will occasionally crash or become unresponsive. Far less common, and much more serious, is hardware failure, which will require you to send the device away for servicing. This chapter gives advice for both situations, along with tips for maximizing battery life and keeping the screen clean.

Crashes and software problems

You should expect, every now and again, your iPad to crash or generally behave in strange ways. This will more often than not be a problem with a specific application, and the iPad will simply throw you out of the app and take you back to the Home Screen. From there, tap your way back to where you were and start again. If the screen completely freezes, however, try force quitting the current application by holding down the Home button for around five or six seconds. If the problem persists, try the following steps, in this order:

• **Reboot** As with any other computer, turning an iPad off and back on often solves software problems. Press and hold the **Sleep/Wake** button for a couple of seconds and then slide the red switch to confirm. Count to five, and then press and hold the **Sleep/Wake** button again to reboot.

• **Reset** If that doesn't do the trick, or you can't get your iPad to turn off, try resetting. This won't harm any music or data on the device. Press and hold the **Sleep/Wake** button and the **Home** button at the same time for around ten seconds. The iPad may first display the regular shutdown screen and red confirm switch; ignore it, and keep holding the buttons, only letting go when the Apple logo appears.

• **Reset all settings** Still no joy? Resetting your iPad's preferences may help. All your current settings will be lost, but no data or media is deleted. Tap **Settings > General > Reset > Reset All Settings**.

• **Erase all content** If that doesn't work, you could try deleting all the media and data, too, by tapping **Settings > General > Reset > Erase All Content and Settings**. Then connect the iPad to your computer and restore your previously backed-up settings and copy all your media back onto the iPad.

• **Restore** This will restore the iPad's software either to the original factory settings or to the settings recorded in the most recent automatic backup. In both cases all data, settings and media are deleted from the device. Connect the iPad to your computer and, within the **Summary** tab of the iPad's options pane, click **Restore** and follow the prompts.

Tip: If you are having problems with Wi-Fi, try tapping the **Reset Network Settings** button on the Reset screen.

iPad firmware

Just as it's always a good idea to run the latest version of iTunes on your Mac or PC, it's worth running the latest version of the iPad's internal software – also known as firmware. The firmware will be automatically updated from time to time when your computer is online and connected to the iPad. This doesn't affect your settings, media or data, but it fixes bugs and will make the iPad run more smoothly.

You can check for new versions at any time by opening iTunes, connecting your iPad and, on the **Summary** screen, clicking **Check for Update**. If a new version is available, install it.

iPad backups

iTunes automatically creates a backup of key data on your iPad whenever you connect to iTunes on your computer. The backup includes mail settings, app preferences, sound settings and more. It doesn't include music, video and other media already duplicated on your computer.

To view, and if necessary delete, an automatic iPad backup, open iTunes **Preferences** and click **Devices**. To restore to a backup, simply connect an iPad and click **Restore** in the iPad .... pane within iTunes.

Of course, the backup – and indeed all your media files – is only as safe as your Mac or PC. Computers can die, get destroyed or be stolen, so get into the habit of backing up to either an external hard drive or writeable DVDs. For more on this subject, see *The Rough Guide to Macs & OS X* and *The Rough Guide to Windows 7*.

The iPad battery

Like all lithium-ion batteries, the one inside the iPad lasts for a certain amount of time before starting to lose its ability to hold a full charge. According to Apple, this reduction in capacity of a "properly maintained" iPad battery will happen after around one thousand "charge cycles" – which, in theory, should give you a good few years of usage, assuming you charge the device on average once a day.

Once the battery has reached the end of its useful life, you can pay to have the battery replaced (though Apple claim that they will in fact replace the entire device). For the full story, see: apple.com/support/ipad/service/battery.

> **Tip:** For Apple's full list of iPad battery preservation tips, visit their website: apple.com/batteries/ipad.html.

If, on the other hand, you drain your battery twice a day by watching movies while commuting to and from work, you might see your battery deteriorate after just nine months or so. In this case, you'd get it replaced for free, as the iPad would still be within warranty.

If the battery won't charge

There has been a fair amount of controversy, and no shortage of misinformation, about issues iPad owners have had trying to charge their devices via a USB port on Macs, PCs and USB hubs. If your iPad won't charge up via a USB port, it could be that the port you're connected to doesn't supply enough power or that your Mac or PC is going into standby mode during the charge.

It has also been reported that iPads will only charge from low-powered USB ports when in sleep mode. To test this hypothesis for your USB port, note the percentage charge on the Status Bar before you connect; then when you see the infuriating "Not charging" message on the iPad's Status Bar, press the Sleep/Wake button to darken the screen and then head to the kettle. Return after a cup of tea, disconnect, and see if the charge has increased.

If you still have no joy, make sure the iPad is okay by trying to charge via the supplied power adapter. If this doesn't work either, it could be the cable; if you have an iPod cable lying around, try that instead, or borrow one from a friend. If you still can't get it to charge, send the iPad for servicing.

Keeping the screen clean

After only a few minutes of using the iPad, it becomes very clear that this is a device that is going to need a lot of wiping and cleaning. The issue is that because the touch screen is designed to repel grease and oil, it simply sits on the service as smeary swipe marks and fingerprints.

The only thing that should be used to wipe the screen is a lint-free cloth, preferably a microfibre one. Every few weeks (depending on your general greasiness) you may wish to wipe clean the screen using the tiniest amount of water (barely enough to dampen the cloth). Do not use any kind of solvents or screen cleaners (even if they claim to be iPad-friendly) – a tiny amount of plain water should do just fine. When you do this, make sure that the iPad is powered off, disconnected from any computers, chargers or other devices, and that no moisture gets near the edge of the bevel or ports and switches.

iPad repairs

If the advice in this chapter hasn't worked, try going online and searching for help on Apple's iPad support pages (apple.com/support/ipad). If that doesn't clear things up, it could be that you'll need to have your iPad repaired by Apple. To do this, you could take it to an Apple retail store, though be warned that in some cases you may have to make an appointment.

Alternatively, visit apple.com/support/service/depot and fill out a service request form. Apple will send you an addressed box in which you can return your iPad to them. For a full list of repair FAQs, visit: apple.com/support/ipad/service/faq.

Part 3

....

Apps

The iTunes App Store

The App Store offers everything from throwaway novelties to fully fledged versions of videogames and "productivity" tools (such as word processors, painting apps and calculators). Though some apps are free, much of this software will cost you a few bucks (payable through your regular iTunes Account) and you can expect to pay, on average, slightly more for an iPad-capable app than for one that runs only on the iPhone (more on this below). The App Store can be accessed in two ways:

• **On the iPad** Tap the **App Store** icon on the iPad's Home Screen to start exploring. Though not a website, the store is online, so you'll need a Wi-Fi or 3G connection to actually get in there to start browsing and downloading the goods.

• **On a Mac or PC** In iTunes, open the iTunes Store via the link in the sidebar and click through to the **Apps** department. Anything you download will be synced across to your iPad next time you connect.

> **Tip:** Different countries have their own iTunes Store, and you can only download apps from the one in the region where your iTunes Account is registered.

The App Store on the iPad looks and works in exactly the same way as the iTunes Store on the iPad – there's a **Featured** section, a search box, and various **Categories** to browse. There's also a button at the bottom of the screen where you can redeem a coupon.

Once you have found an app that interests you, tap to find out more. From here, read reviews (which can be a great indication of an app's worth) or click through to the developer's site. Also keep an eye out for free or "lite" versions of apps that let you try out an app before purchasing the full version.

And before you spend any money on something, think hard, as there are no refunds in the App Store.

iPad and iPhone apps

Not all apps in the App Store are born equal, so to speak, when it comes to the kind of device they will run on. There are basically three flavours that you'll encounter as you browse the store:

• **iPad apps** These are apps that have been designed to run on the iPad, making full use of the available screen real estate. When browsing the App Store from the iPad, these are, not surprisingly, pushed to the fore.

• **iPhone apps** Apple uses this term to describe apps that have been designed to run on their smaller-screened devices – in other words iPhones and the iPod Touch. In most cases they will still work on the iPad, but with the same layout and interface as on a smaller screen. You get to either use the app at its original size, or scaled up to almost fill the iPad's screen (see p.17).

• **Apps designed for both** There are also many apps available that have been designed to run on both iPads and iPhones, but with very different user interfaces. Not to be confused with the scaleable apps mentioned above, these apps might, for example, offer an elegant split-screen interface on the iPad, and a more stripped-down interface on the iPhone. These apps are listed within the App Store displaying a small white **✛** icon.

iTunes Store Accounts

The App Store uses the same iTunes Account credentials as both the iTunes Store and the iBookstore. If you don't already have an account set up, try to download an app in the store and you will quickly be prompted to do so.

What many people don't realize is that neither the iPad, nor iTunes on your computer, have to be wedded to a single iTunes Store Account. So if more than one member of your household uses your iPad (or iTunes on your Mac or PC), there's no reason why you can't all have your own iTunes Store Accounts and buy apps separately. What's more, once apps have been downloaded directly to the iPad they are available for all to use, whichever account is currently logged in to the iPad's Store.

It only becomes an issue when you try to copy apps back to iTunes on a Mac or PC, as this will only work if the computer in question is "authorized" for the Store Account that was used to download the apps. Up to five computers can be authorized for each Store Account. To authorize iTunes for a new account, select **Store > Authorize Computer** and follow the prompts.

You can add apps to multiple iPads, iPhones and iPods from iTunes without having to authorize them or overwrite any apps that might already be installed.

> **Tip:** To log out of your account on the iPad, either tap Settings > **Store > Log Out**, or scroll to the bottom of most App Store windows and tap your **Account: name** button.

Syncing your purchased apps

Apps downloaded from the App Store within iTunes are automatically synced to the iPad next time you connect. But if you want to be more selective about what does and doesn't sync, connect to iTunes, highlight your iPad in the sidebar and then make your selections by checking the boxes under the **Apps** tab.

Apps purchased on the iPad are automatically synced back to iTunes when you connect, assuming that the **Sync Apps** box has been highlighted under the **Apps** tab and your computer has been authorized (see p.99) for the iTunes Account used to purchase the apps.

Checking the settings

Just like the apps that come preinstalled on the iPad, many third-party apps have various preferences and settings available. Many people overlook such options and might end up missing out on certain features as a result. Each app does its own thing, but expect to find something either...

• **In the app** If there is nothing obvious labelled **Options** or **Settings**, look for a cog icon, or perhaps something buried within a **More** menu.

• **In Settings** Tap **Settings** on the Home Screen and scroll down to see if your app has a listing in the left-hand column. Tap it to see what options are available.

Managing apps

Sorting, updating, deleting

Just like with music and video files, iTunes allows you to be selective about which of your apps are synced across to your iPad at any one time. But there's more to iTunes than that: you can also organize the way that your apps appear on the iPad and download updates for your apps as and when they become available.

Apps in iTunes

On both a Mac and PC you can view all the apps you have stored within iTunes at any time by clicking the **Apps** link in the sidebar.

At the top of the iTunes window, there are three buttons that are used to toggle among three separate ways of viewing your apps:

- **List view** This view is the most conservative of the three, but useful for viewing specific info about the size of apps, when they added to iTunes, and so on. Right-click the header bar to bring more info columns into view.

- **Grid view** This view displays all your apps as a grid of icons, arranged alphabetically within device categories… in other

words, all the iPhone-only apps are together, and all the iPad-only apps are together, as are all those that work on both.

• **Cover Flow view** This view has all the handy info of the List view, but with a lovely big area at the top for your app icons (pictured here). To see only the icons, full-screen, click the ▣ button.

> **Tip:** You can rearrange the way your apps appear on the iPad Home Screen from iTunes. For the full story, turn to p.68.

Updating apps

One of the best features of the App Store is that as and when developers release updates for their software, you will automatically be informed of the update and given the option to install it for free, even if you had to shell out for the original download. The number of available updates at any one time is displayed within a red badge on the corner of the App Store's Home Screen icon. To update apps…

• **On the iPad** Choose **App Store > Updates** and then **Update All**. The **Updates** icon at the bottom of the store screen also displays a red badge and number; those that you grab are then synced back to iTunes next time you connect.

> **Tip:** You can also selectively choose which updates you download by tapping the individual **FREE** buttons that appear next to each available item.

• **On a Mac or PC** Highlight **Applications** in the sidebar (where a badge displays the number of available updates) to view all your apps and then click **Check for updates**, bottom-right, to see what's new (pictured here).

Deleting apps

It's worth noting that your iTunes Account keeps a permanent record of which apps you have downloaded, so if you do happen to delete both your iPad's copy and the iTunes copy, you can go back to the Store and download it again at no extra charge. Here's how to delete an app:

• **On the iPad** Hold down any Home Screen icon until they all start jiggling around and then tap the small ⊗ on the corner of the app you want to delete. When you have finished, hit the Pod's Home button. This will not remove the app from iTunes, so you can always sync it back to the iPad again later if you want to.

• **On a Mac or PC** Highlight **Applications** in the iTunes sidebar and then right-click the unwanted app and choose **Delete** from the menu that appears. If the app was also present on the iPad, next time you connect expect a prompt to either remove it from there too, or copy it back into iTunes.

> **Tip:** When asked to rate the app you are deleting, take the opportunity to give it a score out of five; these ratings are then aggregated back into the App Store for the benefit of other users.

Part 4

....

Reading matters

iBooks

Apple's eBook reader and store

For many, the primary reason for buying an iPad is to use it as an eBook reader, and Apple are very much hoping that you will use their iBooks app to do just that, simultaneously giving you access to the Apple iBookstore, from which you can download your tomes.

iBooks is not one of the default apps on the iPad. It is a free app, but you will have to visit the App Store (either on the iPad or from iTunes on your computer) to download it. Unfortunately, not every country has an iBookstore up and running, so if you can't find the iBooks app in your local App Store, it basically means that you are going to have to

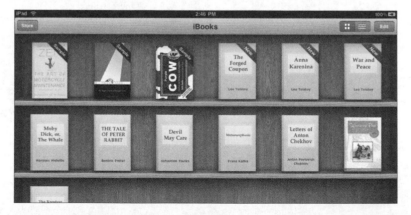

find another means of getting books onto your iPad. (Skip forward to the next chapter to find the answer.)

If you do find the app, once launched it displays either a pretty bookshelf (your Library, where you can browse all your downloaded and synced books) or the iBookstore (which looks very similar to the iPad's iTunes Store). To toggle between the two, tap the button in the top-left corner of the app.

> **Tip:** You can toggle between the "bookshelf" and "list" views of your library using the two buttons on the top-right.

Using the iBookstore

There really aren't any surprises here. You browse books and purchase them in just the same way that you do music, movies and TV shows in the iTunes Store. The iBookstore even uses exactly the same login credentials that you already use in the iTunes Store. Start exploring and you'll quickly get the hang of it.

Sample chapters

In most cases you can tap **Get Sample** to download a free excerpt to whet your appetite. You can download the full text ... ... whilst reading (assuming you are connected to the Internet) by tapping ... ... at the top of any page in the sample.

Reading with the iBooks app

To open a book, simply tap it within your iBooks Library. It either opens to display a single-page view (when the iPad is held in portrait mode) or a spread of two pages (when held in landscape mode). To turn a page, either drag the bottom corner, or tap to the left or right of the text near the edge of the iPad's screen.

> **Tip:** Look within **Settings > iBooks** to determine whether tapping on the left-hand edge takes you to the next page or the previous page.

A single tap anywhere on the body of the page will either reveal or hide further options at the top and bottom (brightness, text options and text search can all be found here).

> **Tip:** Use the slider at the bottom of the page to quickly jump to another part of the book.

• **Contents page** Tap the ▤ button to view the **Contents** page of the title you are reading; once there, tap **Resume** to return to the point where you were reading.

• **Dictionary** Tap and hold any word and choose **Dictionary** from the options bubble to view a full definition (complete with derivatives and the word's origins).

• **Search** Tap and hold any word and choose **Search** from the options bubble; this displays a tappable list of other places where the word occurs in the text and also offers two further links to

Search Google and **Search Wikipedia** (both of which take you out of iBooks and into Safari).

• **VoiceOver** iBooks supports Apple's VoiceOver screen reader, which will read the text aloud for you. Turn it on within **Settings > General > Accessibility**. The voice is, however, a little mechanical for prose, so you may well decide you'd be better off with an audiobook (for more on which, see p.127).

To delete books from your iPad's Library, tap **Edit** and then the ⊗ icon on the title you want to ditch. Assuming it's been synced across already, the title will still be available to sync back again from iTunes next time you connect.

Highlighting and bookmarking

Tap and hold the text you want to highlight and then drag the blur anchor points to adjust the size of the selection. When you are ready, tap **Bookmark**. You can then tap the highlighted text to either change the highlighter colour or **Unbookmark** the selection.

black Mercedes 300D Cabriolet did not
fit in – even here, in a port loud with

| Unbookmark | Yellow | Green | Blue | Pink | Purple |

The car pulled up beside the dock,
where the smaller of the two men, who
wore a short-sleeved
kind of French military kepi, climbed

high chee
straw-colo
driven ba
without a
beige trop
and Whee
scarlet ti
windows
carriagew

To view a list of all the highlighted bookmarks within a given book, tap the ▤ button at the top of the page, and then tap **Bookmarks**. From here you can also delete specific bookmarks from the list by swiping across them and then tapping **Delete**.

> **Tip:** You don't need to bookmark your place when you quit iBooks or exit a book; iBooks remembers where you were and will take you to the same point next time you open the title.

Syncing with iTunes

You can build up a sizeable collection of ePub files on your iPad without having to worry too much about storage space. Text-only books, even very long ones, will only be a couple of megabytes at most (that's about the size of an average digital photo file); titles with lots of images on the other hand can be quite large.

> **Tip:** To keep an eye on how much space books are taking up on your iPad, connect to iTunes and look at the multicoloured status strip at the bottom of the **Summary** panel.

To start syncing your books with iTunes, connect your iPad, select the **Books** tab, and then check the appropriate sync options (pictured). Once this is set up, new iBookstore downloads will be synced back to iTunes every time you connect.

Even though you can't actually read your synced books within iTunes on your computer, it's still a worthwhile exercise as a means of creating a backup of the titles you have downloaded to the iPad.

ePub books from other stores

You can also add DRM-free ePub books not downloaded from the iBookstore to your iPad to read in the iBooks app. To do this, you first need to get them into iTunes on your computer, which is easily done. Highlight the **Books** listing in the iTunes sidebar and then drag and drop the files into the main iTunes window, where they will appear alongside your iBookstore purchases. You can then connect your iPad and sync them across in the normal way.

> **Tip:** If no **Books** listing appears under **Library** in the iTunes sidebar on your computer, open iTunes **Preferences** and check the **Books** box on the **General** pane.

This won't work for Sony Reader Store titles (as they employ a form of DRM), but there are plenty of other ePub sources that can be turned to, including:

• **Smashwords** (smashwords.com) This is a great source for ePub files from independent authors and publishers… the majority of which can't be found in the iBookstore.

• **Google Books** (books.google.com) Plagued by controversy, the Google Books project is an online archive of content that is out of print in the territories where it is made available electronically. Not everything is available to download in ePub format, but there is some interesting stuff to be found.

• **ePubBooks** (epubbooks.com) This excellent site has all the latest eBook news as well as a plethora of ePub titles available for download. Also take a look at their links page (epubbooks.com/buy-epub-books) for shortcuts to buy ePub files from both online retailers and direct from publishers such as Penguin, Mills & Boon, and many more.

There are plenty of other sites and services out there, but be warned, just because a website is offering to sell you books in the ePub format, it doesn't mean they are legitimate dealers passing on the appropriate cut to publishers and authors. It's often worth going straight to the publisher's site to find out who distributes their files.

Rolling your own

Whether you are an author yourself, a student, or someone who simply wants to view and organize text documents within the iBooks app, there are loads of benefits to being able to create your own ePub files to use with the iPad.

Many of the industry-standard publishing software packages (such as Adobe's InDesign) make the creation of ePub files very easy indeed, but are prohibitively expensive for most mere mortals. There are plenty of cheaper and more specialized alternatives, however, including:

• **Storyist** (storyist.com) This piece of Mac-only software does a fantastic job of crafting ePub files. The interface is intuitive and there are various automated functions that make the whole thing a doddle, all for around the price of a decent meal for two (with wine).

• **eCub** (juliansmart.com/ecub) This no-frills package is available free for both Mac and PC and can help you bash out a few ePub files in no time. It even includes tools for creating cover art for your titles.

• **Sigil** (code.google.com/p/sigil) Another free, multi-platform offering can be found under Google's umbrella. The interface and tools are excellent, so much so that it can be used as a general word processor as well as an ePub cruncher.

If you are looking for a way to read ePub files on your Mac or PC, try the free-to-use Adobe Digital Editions (adobe.com/products/digitaleditions).

Other ways to read

iPad reading beyond iBooks

iBooks is not your only option for reading eBooks on the iPad. And what's more, the ePub format is all well and good for fiction, but not so hot when it comes to highly illustrated publications, such as comics, many kids' books, and picture-heavy reference titles. For these you are more than likely going to find what you want in the App Store rather than the iBookstore.

eBook reading apps

As already mentioned, there are plenty of alternatives to iBooks for eBook reading. Take a look in the App Store's **Books** category and you'll find no shortage of individual titles that have been converted to apps. More interestingly, however, there are also many eBook reader apps that give you access to extensive online catalogues to browse, download and read:

• **Kindle** For those who want to purchase their reading material from Amazon, the free Kindle app gives you access to all the same Kindle files that you read on either your Kindle device or desktop Kindle application. Files are pushed to your iPad over the airwaves by Amazon's Whispersync technology, and though you can't access the Amazon Kindle Store from the app, once you make a purchase via Amazon.com, the file pops up on the iPad almost instantaneously.

• **Stanza** This reader/store does a similar job to the iBooks app. There are thousands of titles available (via Project Gutenberg, and links to various different stores) and you can also add your own ePub, eReader, PDF and Mobipocket titles using the Stanza Desktop application (available for both Mac and PC from lexcycle.com).

> **Tip:** You can also get free classics direct from the Project Gutenberg archive website (gutenberg.org).

• **Kobo** Nice-looking app that gives you access to thousands of titles from the Kobo store. The reading experience is also excellent, with font and bookmarking options, as well as a very useful white-on-black night reading mode.

Books as apps

General reference

Either search the App Store by keyword or start browsing the **Books** category. There are some amazing apps on offer, but in most cases you get what you pay for and, generally, the most inspiring apps retail for roughly the same price as a good book. A few worth shelling out for:

• **The Elements** All the info you could want on the stuff that makes up the universe. The interactive graphics (pictured here) make it both entertaining and educational.

• **Carter's Encyclopedia of Health and Medicine** Beautifully presented; amazing graphics and diagrams; essential reading for anyone with a general interest in how the body works.

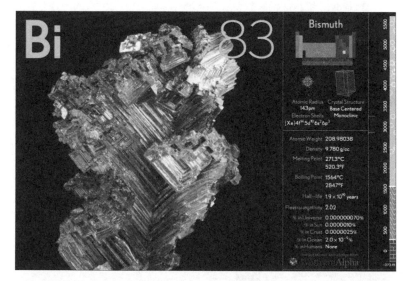

• **Phaidon Design Classics** An amazing re-imagining for the iPad of the weighty three-volume bestselling tome on product design.

Comics and graphic novels

As you might imagine, graphic novels and comics are fantastic to read on the iPad, and the list of available titles grows week by week.

• **Marvel** Access to an essential store of classic superhero comics. Download and read either page by page or frame by frame.

• **iVerse Comics** A really easy-to-use store and comic reader. There are both paid-for and free comics to be found here covering all genres and ages of reader.

• **iMangaX** Over a thousand manga to browse and read. All the content is stored online, so an Internet connection is essential.

Kids' reading

If you have young children you will already have realized that it's pretty hard to keep them away from the iPad. Here's a couple of kids' books to keep them entertained:

• **The Cat In the Hat** Beautifully re-created for the screen, you can read it like a book, listen to the narrative, or play the whole thing through like a movie.

• **iReadingHD** A company that produces many kids' reading books available in the store. The Cover Flow mode allows you to quickly jump between favourite pages and you can touch each character to hear them make a sound. If you want to leave your toddler alone with your iPad, turn on Auto Narration and let them get on with it.

Dealing with PDFs

As already mentioned, the iPad can deal with PDFs straight out of the box, assuming that they are being viewed from either an email attachment in Mail, or via a web link in Safari. There are, however, also several dedicated PDF reader apps in the App Store... useful if you want your electronic books in PDF rather than other eBook formats:

• **PDF Reader Pro** A fully featured PDF reader and sync tool that lets you either grab PDFs from the web or move them across from your computer using the File Sharing features on the **Apps** panel within iTunes (pictured).

• **GoodReader** Another very useful PDF reader app, but one that can also handle text files, PowerPoint presentations and numerous other formats. It can sync over Wi-Fi, via the iTunes File Sharing tools, and also via connections to cloud storage services such as MobileMe, Google Docs and Dropbox.

• **ReaddleDocs** Like GoodReader, this is a great all-round PDF storage and reading tool. The interface for browsing your files is particularly nice, and it allows you to open attachments into its reader directly from the iPad Mail app.

Part 5

....

Music and video

iTunes

Preparing music and video files to sync with the iPad

Downloading music and video from the iTunes Store (either direct to the iPad or to your computer) is all well and good, but if you already own the CD or DVD, there's no point in paying for the same content again. "Ripping" CDs and DVDs to get them into iTunes (and in turn onto the iPad) is easy, but it's worth reading through this chapter even if you've done it hundreds of times, as various preferences and features are easy to miss.

Importing CDs

To get started, insert any audio CD into your Mac or PC. In most cases, within a few seconds you'll find that the artist, track and album names – and maybe more info besides – automatically appear. If your song info fails to materialize (and all you get is "Track 1", "Track 2", etc), or you want to edit what has appeared, either click into individual fields and type, or select multiple tracks and choose **File > Get Info** to make your changes.

Settings and importing

Before importing all your music, have a look through the various importing options, which you'll find behind the **Import Settings** button on the **General** pane of **iTunes Preferences**. These are worth considering early on, as they relate to sound quality and compatibility. The iPad can play MP3 and AAC files (up to 320Kbps) as well as Apple Lossless, AIFF, Audible and WAV files.

The bitrate is the amount of data that each second of sound is reduced to. The higher the bitrate, the higher the sound quality, but also the more space the file takes up. The relationship between file size and bitrate is basically proportional, but the same isn't true of sound quality, so a 128Kbps track takes half as much space as a 256Kbps version, but the sound will be only marginally different.

> **Tip:** To rip multiple tracks as one, simply select them and click **Advanced > Join CD Tracks** before you import.

Take a quick look at the other options on offer, but don't worry too much as the defaults will do just fine. That said, the iPad only has a mono speaker (but does have a stereo headphone jack), so if capacity is an issue you could rip mono versions of your songs to use on it – they'll take up half the space of stereo versions.

When you are ready to import, hit the Import button in the bottom-right corner of the iTunes window.

Importing DVDs

Just as with music, before you can transfer video files to your iPad, you first have to get them into iTunes. In most cases, it's perfectly possible to do this from DVD, though in some countries this may not be strictly legal when it comes to copyrighted movies. As long as you're only importing your own DVDs for your own use, no one is likely to mind. The main problem is that it's a bit of a hassle. A DVD contains so much data that it can take more than an hour to "rip" each movie to your computer in a format that'll work with iTunes and an iPad. And if the disc contains copy protection, then it's even more of a headache.

Tip: Some DVDs feature promotional codes that entitle you to a free iTunes digital version of the same movie.

DVD copy protection

DVDs are often encrypted, or copy protected, to stop people making copies or ripping the discs to their computers. PC owners can use a program such as AnyDVD (slysoft.com) to get around the protection, while Mac owners trying to get encrypted DVDs into iTunes will need to grab a program such as Fast DVD Copy (fastdvdcopy.com). This allows you to make a non-protected copy of the movie, which you can then turn into an iPad-formatted version using HandBrake. Note that, in some countries, it may not be legal to copy an encrypted DVD.

Of the various free tools available for getting DVDs into iTunes, probably the best is HandBrake, which is available for both Mac and PC. Here's how the process works:

• **Download and install HandBrake** from handbrake.fr.

• **Insert the DVD** and, if it starts to play automatically, quit your DVD player program.

• **Launch HandBrake** and it should detect the DVD (it may call it something unfriendly like "/dev/rdisk1"). Press **Open**, and wait until the application has scanned the DVD.

• **Choose iPad-friendly settings** Choose either the **iPad** or **Apple TV** options from the **Presets** menu.

• **Check the source** It's also worth taking a quick look at the **Title** dropdown menu within the **Source** section of HandBrake. Choose the one that represents the largest amount of time (say 01h22m46s) as this should be the main feature. If nothing of an appropriate length appears, then your DVD is copy protected.

> **Tip:** Ripping Blu-ray discs is at present a prohibitively complex and time-consuming process (possible only with a PC). Better to hunt out discs that come with an accompanying digital version on DVD.

• **Subtitles** If it's a foreign-language film, set **Dialogue** and **Subtitles** options from the dropdown menus behind the **Audio & Subtitles** tab.

• **Rip** Hit the **Start** button at the bottom of the window and the encoding will begin. Don't hold your breath.

• **Drop the file into iTunes** Unless you choose to save it somewhere else, the file will eventually appear on the Desktop. Drag the file into the main iTunes window. This should create a copy of the new file in your iTunes Library allowing you to then delete the original file from your Desktop.

> **Tip:** To learn about importing from other music and video sources, see *The Rough Guides to iPods & iTunes*.

Converting files in iTunes

If you find yourself with music or video files in iTunes that can't be copied across to the iPad when you sync (perhaps they are of the wrong file type or, in the case of music files, have too high a bitrate), you can easily convert them to an iPad-friendly format.

To do this for a video file, select it within iTunes and choose **Advanced > Create iPad or Apple TV**. In the case of an audio file, the option is determined by the **Import Settings** that you define within iTunes Preferences. So, for example, if iTunes is set to import files as MP3, you will be offered the option to **Create MP3 Version** within the **Advanced** menu.

Supported video formats

Getting technical for a moment, the various video formats that the iPad supports include:

• **H.264-encoded video** up to 720p at 30 frames per second, with AAC-LC audio up to 160Kbps, 48kHz, in m4v, mp4 and mov formats.

• **MPEG-4** up to 640x480 pixels, 2.5Mbps, with AAC-LC audio up to 160Kbps, 48kHz.

• **Motion JPEG (M-JPEG)** Avi-wrapped and up to 1280x720 pixels, 35Mbps, 30 frames per second with ulaw PCM stereo audio. (This is the video format often used by digital cameras that can take video.)

If you find that you have files on your computer that don't meet these criteria, either convert them within iTunes or use HandBrake, as previously described.

Managing files in iTunes

Once you start digging around within the **Music** and **Movies** sync tabs of iTunes it will soon become clear that the easiest way to manage your content for syncing to the iPad is by using playlists:

• **Regular playlists** To create a new playlist, hit the **New Playlist** button (the **+**) at the bottom-left of the iTunes window. You can drag individual songs into the new list or add entire albums, artists or genres in one fell swoop. You can also create a new playlist by dragging songs, artists, albums or genres directly onto some blank space in the playlist area, or by selecting a bunch of material and choosing **File > New Playlist**.

•Smart Playlists Rather than being compiled manually by you, these are put together by iTunes according to a set of rules, or "conditions", that you define. It might be songs with a certain word in their title, or a set of genres, or the tracks you've listened to the most – or a combination of any of these kinds of things. The clever thing about Smart Playlists is that their contents will automatically change over time, as relevant tracks are added to your Library or existing tracks meet the criteria by being, say, rated highly. To create a new Smart Playlist, look in the **File** menu or click the **New Playlist** button while holding down **Alt** (Mac) or **Shift** (PC) – you'll see the **+** button change into a cog.

Once you have all your audio and video files organized and ready to sync, connect your iPad to your computer and check the boxes for the content you want to move across within the **Music**, **Movies** and **TV Shows** tabs of iTunes.

Audio on the iPad

iPod, Remote and other apps

The iPad doesn't feel like the most obvious personal music system in the world. You certainly aren't going to go out jogging with it tucked under your arm; and if you simply want a device for listening to music or podcasts on the move, a regular iPod will serve your needs well enough. That said, the iPad's speaker is surprisingly powerful, and the available tools – both from Apple and third-party apps – are pretty compelling.

The iPad's iPod

The iPad's built-in iPod app looks great, is easy to use, and is your one-stop shop for playing music, podcasts, audio books and music videos (which also appear within the iPad's Videos app). Tap the iPod icon on the Dock to start.

Take a look at the row of view options at the bottom of the main listings screen. The **Albums** layout is arguably the most pleasing, as it makes full use of any album artwork

associated with your files. From there on in, it really is
pretty self-explanatory: tap to see listings and then tap a
track to hear it. You can also tap the **Now Playing** area at
the bottom of the left-hand column to enter the full-screen
"Now Playing" mode.

Tapping reveals or hides specific controls, and the ◀
button takes you back to your listings view. You might also
want to try...

• **Scrubbing** To rewind or fast-forward within a song, slide
the progress dot on the "scrubber" bar to the left or right.
Alternatively, press and hold the ◀◀ and ▶▶ controls.

> **Tip:** Slide your finger up and down the screen to adjust the rate of
> the scrubbing; this feature works for video playback too.

• **Adjust the volume** This is done from either the buttons on the side of the iPad, or the ◀)) slider within the iPod app.

• **Shuffle** From the "Now Playing" screen tap the ⤬ icon to turn the shuffle selection feature on (blue) or off (white).

• **Repeat** The iPod app offers two repeat modes, which are available via the ⇄ icon on the "Now Playing" screen. Tap it once (it goes blue) to play the current selection of songs round and round forever. Tapping it again (⇄) repeats just the current track.

• **Genius** This feature generates a list of songs from your collection based upon accumulated iTunes Store information. In short, the Genius algorithms recognize that, for example, people who like The Beatles may well also like The Rolling Stones. Tap the ※ icon to start – this will base the list on the currently playing song, or, if nothing is playing, prompt you to choose a song to define the list

• **Create a playlist** From the main listings screen, tap the + button and follow the prompts, using the ⊕ icons to add individual songs. To edit playlists, select one in the left-hand column, tap **Edit**, and then use the ⊖ icons to remove items, and the draggable ≡ icons to change the order of the list.

> **Tip:** Playlists you create on the iPad will be synced back to iTunes next time you connect.

• **Star ratings** From the "Now Playing" screen, tap the ▤ icon and then slide your finger across the row of dots below the scrubber bar to add a rating for the currently playing selection.

> **Tip:** Sync the music on your iPad from iTunes using a Smart Playlist of five-star ratings; you can then swiftly remove tracks you don't want by changing their rating on the iPad.

• **Home button controls** Once music is playing, you can exit the iPod app and continue to listen whilst using other apps. If you work like this a lot, it's worth setting up your Home button so that a double-tap gives you quick access to the iPod's controls. Do this under **Settings > General > Home**.

> **Tip:** For EQ, Sound Check and Volume Limit controls for iPod playback on the iPad, tap through from the Home Screen to **Settings > iPod**.

The spoken word

If the spoken word is your thing, the iPod app is the place to go to play podcasts and audiobooks on the iPad. Playback works in a similar way as it does with music, although you have a couple of different options available to you from the "Now Playing" screen:

• **Tell a friend (podcasts only)** Tap the ✉ icon to send an email link to a friend so that they can find the podcast you are listening to in the iTunes Store.

• **Backtrack 30 seconds** Tapping the **30** icon, bottom-centre, will rewind the audio by thirty seconds.

• **Playback speed** To adjust the playback speed of your audiobook or podcast, tap the **1x** icon to the right of the scrubber bar (to choose either **2x** or **½x**).

> **Tip:** To load up with audiobooks and podcasts, visit the iTunes Store, either from your iPad or computer.

Remote controls

For many users, the iPad quickly shows itself to be an excellent "couch" device – great for a bit of web surfing or email without having to sit in front of a full-sized computer. As such, it's also great as a remote control for any number of audio – and video – setups:

• **Apple Remote** Free to download from the App Store, Apple's Remote app can be used on the iPad to control iTunes on your computer via Wi-Fi. Coupled with an Apple Airport Express unit, this can be a great way to stream music from a computer in the bedroom, say, to your hi-fi system in the living room. Once set up, you may well find that for domestic use it negates any need to sync music to your iPad at all. It also works with an Apple TV unit connected to your television, allowing you to move around the onscreen menu system (pictured here) by swiping and tapping on the iPad's screen. For the full story on the Remote app, visit apple.com/itunes/remote, and for more on the Apple TV, point your browser at apple.com/appletv.

• **Rowmote Pro** Though it'll cost you a few dollars, this super-charged remote control app is well worth having a play with as it gives you access to all sorts of applications on your computer (Macs only at the time of writing), not just iTunes. It's especially useful if you have your computer connected to the television in your living room, allowing you to perform all sorts of tasks from the comfort of your sofa. (Diet and exercise regime not included.)

Apps for listening to music

Aside from the iPad's built-in iPod, there are plenty of other apps that'll let you listen to music… assuming you can connect to the Internet.

• **Spotify** With this app and a Premium Spotify account, you can stream unlimited music to your iPad from the Internet each month for around the price of a CD album. Though not yet available in many countries, including the US, it's a pretty compelling offering for those who can get it.

• **AccuRadio** There are plenty of Internet radio players to be found in the App Store; this one is free, has an easy-to-use interface, and lets you create favourites lists.

• **Pandora** Only available in the US, this well-established Internet radio service has the added twist of personal recommendations based on your taste.

> **Tip:** To instantly identify songs using the iPad's microphone, try the **SoundHound** or **Shazam** apps.

Apps for making music

The Music category within the iTunes App Store is awash with virtual instruments, sequencers, drum pads and other noisy creations that, in the hands of most people, will make you want to stuff fistfuls of cotton wool into your ears. With a bit of perseverance and a sprinkling of talent, however, there are some that can be made to sound more than just a novelty. Here's a few worth looking at:

• **Air Harp** When the iPhone App Store was launched the world was wowed by virtual guitar apps. Now we have the iPad... more screen, more strings. This is a great fun app, complete with notation sheets so that you can learn some pretty ditties.

• **Looptastic HD** Amazing dance-music creation tool, with nine hundred built-in loops and the ability to add your own. There's also a bunch of effects and time-stretch tools.

• **Korg iElectribe** Arguably the best sequencer and tone generator for the iPad, with a delightful analogue feel to the interface.

• **Sheets** A massive collection of classical sheet music in a single app, all beautifully rendered on the iPad's screen. (Getting the thing to balance on a music stand might be a bit of a challenge though.)

> **Tip:** Remember that the headphone jack can be used as a line-out to play y̶ ̶ ̶ ̶ ̶ ̶tions via a PA, amplifier or hi-fi system instead of the iPad's built-in speaker.

Video on the iPad

Movies, TV shows, YouTube

The iPad's screen is great for watching video: it's not so small that the image is a strain to watch, but the device is also not so big that it can't be snuggled up with in bed to watch a movie or even propped up in the kitchen while you cook along to a recipe podcast.

Playing videos

Unlike on other Apple devices, where the iPod app also plays videos, the iPad has its own dedicated app called, er, Videos. Straight out of the box you'll find it on the Home Screen. Depending what content you have either downloaded from the iTunes Store or synced across from iTunes, within this app you'll find category tabs for **Movies**, **TV Shows**, **Podcasts** and **Music Videos**.

Tap an itcm to find out more, and then hit the ▶ button to start playback. Once the video is playing, tapping the screen reveals play, volume and scrubbing controls. Also

note the icon to the right of the scrubber bar, which can be used to toggle between theatrical widescreen and full-screen (cropped) views.

> **Tip:** You can also toggle between the two view modes by simply double-tapping the screen.

To delete a movie from the iPad after viewing (which can be really handy if you want to make space for more content when out and about), simply tap and hold its thumbnail in the videos list until the ⊗ icon appears at its corner. Tap that and the movie vanishes, though it will still be in iTunes should you want to watch it again.

> **Tip:** Tap the "speech bubble" icon next to the play ~~~~ audio and subtitles options for the playing movie.

Video out

The iPad can output both NTSC and PAL TV signals (select the one you want within **Settings > Video**) so that you can connect your iPad to a TV or projector. This can be done using one of the following, which all attach to the iPad via the Dock connector:

• **Apple iPad Dock Connector to VGA Adapter** This is great for connecting to most projectors when giving presentations.

• **Apple Component AV Cable** This gives you five RCA-style plugs: three for the video and two for the audio.

• **Apple Composite AV Cable** This gives you three RCA-style plugs: one for the video and two for the audio.

These accessories need to be purchased separately from Apple. Many third-party manufacturers make cheaper versions, which should work with the iPad, assuming they have the appropriate Dock connector, though it's always worth checking with the manufacturer before you buy, as some Dock connector cables and adapters may only work with older iPods or iPhones.

Also, be warned, the TV-out signal from the iPad does not simply mirror the iPad's screen, and only works with certain apps (such as **Videos**, **YouTube** and **Keynote**), so don't assume it's going to work with everything.

Tip: For additional video playback options and settings, look within Settings > Video.

YouTube

The iPad comes with a dedicated YouTube app, which can be used to access all the content from YouTube (assuming you are connected to the Internet). The playback controls work in exactly the same way as the Videos app, though here you can watch videos either in full-screen mode or in a browser-like mode (pictured here). To move between the two views, tap the  and  buttons.

Tip: If you see no video controls, tap the playing video to reveal them; this works in both full-screen and browser views.

Explore the various options on offer: you can **Share** (send a link by email), **Rate** (out of five) or **Flag** (if you find the clip offensive) individual clips and also sign in using a YouTube account login (Google account logins also work) allowing you to access your uploads, subscriptions and favourites.

Streaming TV

Sure, you can purchase pretty much any TV season you fancy from the iTunes Store, but there are also many streaming TV services that work on the iPad (even though it lacks Flash). The main limitations to watching either live or catch-up TV on the iPad are regional: many services that are currently accessible in Europe aren't in the US, and vice versa. You are sure to find some that work, but don't be too surprised if a few of the below apps and websites dish you up a whole lot of nothing.

- **ABC Player** (app) Many of the big-name US shows under one roof: *Desperate Housewives*, *Lost*, etc.

- **Netflix** (app) A very slick app for streaming content through your US Netflix account. It works via both Wi-Fi and 3G.

- **TVCatchup** (tvcatchup.com) The only thing you need to stream live UK TV to the iPad for free through Safari.

- **At Bat 2010** (app) Live US Major League Baseball with onscreen stats.

- **Boxee** (app) Though not released at the time of writing, the Boxee app is rumoured to be in the pipe, so check the App Store, or for their latest news, visit boxee.tv.

The iTunes Store

Buying and renting, direct from the iPad

The iTunes Store isn't the only option for downloading music and video from the Internet. But if you use the iPad, it's unquestionably the most convenient, offering instant, legal access to millions of music tracks, plus a growing selection of TV shows and movies to either buy or rent. Unlike some download stores, the iTunes Store is not a website, so don't expect to reach it with Safari – the only way in is via the iTunes icon on the iPad's Home Screen.

What have they got?

At the time of writing, the iTunes Store boasts more than eleven million tracks worldwide, plus twenty thousand audiobooks and many thousands of movies and TV shows. It claims to have the largest legal download catalogue in the world.

iTunes Accounts

Though anyone can browse the iTunes Store on the iPad, listen to samples and watch previews and movie trailers, if you actually want to buy anything you need to set up an account and be logged in. If you haven't already done this, it's easily done: either try and buy something, and follow the prompts, or head to **Settings > Store** and enter the necessary details there.

> **Tip:** If you already have an Apple ID, MobileMe Account or iBookstore login, exactly the same credentials will work here; you can also use an AOL account if you have one.

If someone else is already signed in to the Store on the same iPad, they'll need to sign out first within **Settings > Store**. Also note that iTunes Store Accounts are country-specific; in other words, you only get to access the store of the country where the credit card associated with the account has a registered billing address.

Staying secure

By default the iPad will remember your details, making purchasing content all too easy. This could be asking for trouble (especially if you have kids around). It's safer to only enter your password each time you want to buy something, remembering to log out when you're done (scroll to the bottom of any iTunes Store listings page and tap the **Account: yourname** button). Alternatively, use a passcode (**Settings > General > Passcode Lock**) to control who has access to your iPad and the shopping opportunities therein.

> **Tip:** If you want to stop your kids either accessing the Store entirely or being exposed to explicit material, look for the options under **Settings > General > Restrictions**.

Renting movies

Many of the major movie studios are now making their films (both new releases and catalogue titles) available for rental via the iTunes Store. Some titles are additionally available in high definition (HD) with a slightly higher rental cost. Once a rented movie file has been downloaded to your iPad you have 30 days to start watching it, and once you have played even just a few seconds of the file, you have a certain period of time to finish it (in the US it's 24 hours, in the UK, 48). When your time runs out the file miraculously disappears.

A movie rented on the iPad can't then be transferred to a computer or other device to be watched there. You can, however, rent a movie through iTunes on a Mac or PC and then sync it across to the iPad.

Annoyingly, you need to fully download a movie before you can start watching it, which, depending on your

Internet connection, could take a few hours. To see how your download is progressing, tap the **Downloads** button at the bottom of the iTunes Store window.

More in the Store

New features are added to the iTunes Store on a regular basis. Here's a list of a few other things that you might like to explore.

- **Redeeming gift cards** If you are lucky enough to have been given one, you can use iTunes Store gift cards and certificates to pay for content in the Store. To redeem a gift, tap **Music**, scroll down, tap **Redeem** and follow the prompts. Your store credit then appears with your account info at the bottom of most iTunes Store screens.

- **iTunes U** iTunes U ("university") makes available lectures, debates and presentations from US colleges as audio and video files. The service is free and has made unlikely stars of some of the more entertaining professors.

- **Freebies** Keep an eye open for free tracks: you get something for nothing, and you might discover an artist you never knew you liked.

- **Genius** Tap the **Genius** tab to get movie, TV show and music recommendations based upon items you've already bought.

> **Tip:** Purchases sync back to iTunes on your computer when you ... ... can be viewed in the **Purchased on...** playlist that appears in the iTunes sidebar.

DRM and authorized computers

All tracks in the iTunes Store come without traditional built-in DRM (Digital Rights Management) of the kind that Apple used to use to stop content being copied and passed on. Without the built-in DRM there are no technological barriers to someone distributing the files they have purchased. However, files downloaded from the iTunes Store do contain the purchaser's name and email details embedded as "metadata" within the file. The upshot of this is that files purchased from iTunes and then illegally distributed over the Internet are traceable back to the person who originally shelled out for them. The other thing worth noting about iTunes-purchased files is that they're in the AAC format, so they'll only play in iTunes, on iPods, iPhones, iPads and any non-Apple software and hardware that supports this type of file; unless, of course, you convert them to MP3 first (see p.124).

Apple also use what's known as FairPlay DRM, where content purchased using a specific iTunes Account can only be played on (or synced to, in the case of books and apps) a maximum of five Macs or PCs that are "authorized" for that account. (You can, however, add content to as many iPads, iPods and iPhones as you want; you just won't be able to move it onto a Mac or PC that has not been authorized.)

To manage the machines authorized for your iTunes Account, open iTunes on your Mac or PC and look for the options in the **Store** menu. To deauthorize all machines and start afresh (useful if you no longer have access to one or more of your five), choose **Store > View My Account > Deauthorize All**.

....

Part 6

Photos on the iPad

Organizing and viewing

The iPad is a great tool for carrying around your images and showing them off to all and sundry. Unlike a laptop, as soon as you start flicking through images on the screen, it stops feeling like a computing device and instead takes on the guise of an interactive picture frame that anyone can learn how to use in seconds. And even though the first-generation iPads don't have a camera built in, there are several ways to get fresh pictures onto the device when on the move, making it perfect for dumping the contents of your digital camera while on vacation.

Putting pictures on an iPad

Syncing with iTunes

The iPad can be loaded up with images from your computer. iTunes moves them across, in the process creating copies that are optimized for the iPad's screen, thereby minimizing the disk space they occupy. You shouldn't have any trouble with image formats, as all the most common (JPEG, TIFF, GIF, PNG and RAW) are supported. iTunes can sync photos and videos with any folder on your computer that contains images or videos or from one of three supported photo-management tools:

- **iPhoto** (Mac; version 4.0.3 or later; apple.com/iphoto) This application is part of Apple's iLife package, which is free with all new Macs (and available separately for $79).

- **Aperture** (Mac; version 3.0.2 or later; apple.com/aperture) This is Apple's professional digital camera application. It's an impressive piece of software for the money ($199), but does way more than most people would need.

- **Photoshop Elements** (PC; version 3.0 or later; adobe.com/photoshopelements) This application is similar to iPhoto, but with far more editing tools and a $90 price tag.

All these applications offer editing tools for colour balance and so on, and allow you to arrange your images into "albums", which will show up on the iPad. If you prefer, though, you can keep your photos within a standard folder, such as the **My Pictures** folder in Windows, or the **Pictures** folder in OS X. Any sub-folders will be treated as albums.

To copy across your photos, connect your iPad to your computer and look under the Photos tab in iTunes. Check the sync box then choose your application or folder. If your images are elsewhere use the **Choose Folder** option to browse for them. Scroll down the panel to choose Albums, sub-folders and other options. When you are ready, hit **Apply** to sync your additions.

> **Tip:** Note that as you check boxes to add selections, the number of images that you are adding to be synced appears to the right of the item you have checked.

Importing from an iPhone or digital camera

To do this you are going to have to pick up the iPad Camera Connection Kit (which Apple sell for $29), which features two adapters. The first allows you to connect your iPhone or digital camera directly to the iPad's Dock connector using a USB cable (you are basically paying for a regular USB port), while the second is for inserting an SD memory card of the type found in many digital cameras.

Once you have made the connection the Photos application will launch and show you all the photos that are available to import.

> **Tip:** If nothing happens, make sure your camera or phone is turned on, and if it has a special "import" mode, activate it.

Either tap **Import All** or tap to select the ones you want, and then tap **Import**. When the import process has finished you can choose to either keep or delete the photos on the SD card, camera or iPhone. To view the new photos, look in either **Albums > Last Import** or **Events > Today's date**.

> **Tip:** You can transfer photos back to your computer from the iPad just as you would from a digital camera or phone (using an application such as iPhoto or Photoshop Elements, for example).

Other ways to import

There are several other ways to get pictures into the Photos app on an iPad. In all these instances, a new album appears named **Saved Photos**.

• **From the web** Tap and hold any image on a webpage in Safari and choose **Save Image** from the options bubble.

• **From an attachment** Tap and hold any image within an email and choose **Save Image** from the options bubble.

• **From an iPhone's camera** Download **Camera** for the App Store and take photos from an iPhone, saving them onto the iPad via Wi-Fi or Bluetooth.

Viewing images on the iPad

The Photos app makes great use of the iPad's screen real estate and has several neat features. Once your images are on the iPad, photo navigation is straightforward. Tap **Albums** to see your images arranged as stacks, or tap **Photos** to see the images in all albums laid out as a grid. To preview an album's contents, slowly stretch the stack with two fingers.

When viewing either an album or all your photos, tapping the 🖃 button allows you to tap and select multiple images to then either email or copy. When viewing all photos, you can also delete images.

Once viewing an individual image, you can…

- **Swipe left and right** to move to the previous or next photo.

- **Zoom in and out** Double-tap or "stretch" and "pinch" with two fingers.

- **Rotate the iPad** to see the picture in either landscape or portrait mode.

• **Flip the iPad** to show the image to someone facing you... they will see the picture the right way up.

• **Hide or reveal the controls** Tap once anywhere on the image.

• **Share the photo** Tap 🖃 to either email the image or post it to a MobileMe gallery (see box overleaf). Tapping 🖃 also displays options for assigning a pic to a contact, setting it as your Lock or Home Screen wallpaper, or copying it, ready to be pasted elsewhere.

> **Tip:** If you tap and hold an image within either the **Photos** view, or a specific album, you also get the option to **Copy** from there.

Slideshows

To kick-start a slideshow, open an album and tap **Slideshow**, choose from various options on the popover menu; when you are ready, tap **Start Slideshow**. You can also connect to a TV (see p.248) to play your slideshows.

> **Tip:** For more slideshow options, tap through to **Settings > Photos** from the iPad's Home Screen.

Faces and Places

These are two features that show up on the iPad when you sync images across from a Mac using a recent version of iPhoto. It basically allows you to view your library of images grouped in terms of the people in the shot (Faces) or presented as locations on a map (Places).

MobileMe and the Gallery app

To post images directly from the iPad to MobileMe, simply tap the ✉ button and follow the prompts, choosing which of your existing MobileMe albums (which you can set up via the web at me.com/gallery) you want to publish to.

Though arguably more useful on the iPhone than the iPad, there is also a MobileMe **Gallery** app available from the App Store, which can be used to view MobileMe albums online – both your own and those that you've been sent links to. For the latter to work, tap **Settings > Configure Safari for Gallery** within the app, so that MobileMe links are redirected to the app instead of Safari.

To get started with Faces, select any image in iPhoto on your Mac and hit the **Name** button on the lower toolbar. Next, click **Add Missing Face** to identify people in the shot. Then click **Faces** in the sidebar and double-click the Polaroid-style preview to discover that iPhoto has attempted to identify every other image in your library featuring the same face. Clever stuff. Then, connect your iPad, and under the **Photos** tab in iTunes, scroll down and check the boxes next to the names that you want to add to the iPad. When you're done, hit **Apply**.

As for Places (pictured here), if you take photos using either a camera or phone with GPS (global positioning system) capabilities, this information will be embedded in the image file and allows Photos on the iPad to show you the exact location the image was snapped. Tap the **Places**

tab and then tap any of the red pins to see the images that were taken in that location.

Flickr on the iPad

Flickr, the world's most popular photo-sharing site, also works well with an iPad. There are various apps that can be downloaded from the App Store to manage your Flickr collection and sync images to the iPad so that you have access to them offline. Two worth trying are **flickr Photos** and the excellent, though rather over-monikered, **Photo Pad: Flickr - Sync Photos**.

Getting creative

Drawing, painting and tweaking

Who needs pens and pencils when you have a finger? The iPad section of the App Store is awash with amazing pieces of software that allow you to sketch, daub, smear and splatter away to your heart's content. So whether you are looking to produce something professional-looking or simply to distract the kids for a few hours, there's an app out there for you. Take a look in the App Store to see what you can find. Searching either "paint" or "draw" will yield more apps than you might know what to do with, so here's a few recommendations to get you started.

Brushes

Brushes is a beautifully crafted app that artists of any level will have a lot of fun with. It supports image layering, different brush textures and weights, and the ability to control the transparency and weight of your strokes based

on the speed with which you move your finger. Also present is a very cool "replay" feature that lets you watch the progress of your creation as a movie once you're done.

You can also import images from Photos on the iPad to incorporate into your artwork.

SketchBook Pro

Like Brushes, this app supports layers and is really intuitive to use. Overall, it is an offering more suited to professional use, and has loads of tools, brushes and textures, and an incredible zoom feature, which allows you to get right in there and add detail.

Filterstorm

For all your image and photo adjustment needs, try this app. It allows you to load images from your Photos library and then subtly mess around with various settings and curves (hue, luminance, etc). There's also a bunch of photographic effects that can be added (vignette, sharpen, blur, and so on). The end results are deposited in your Saved Photos album, so you don't risk doing any damage to the originals.

123 Color HD

There are loads of colouring apps aimed specifically at kids. This one is a real treat – it has songs, voiceovers and multiple languages built in (so can be used for basic language teaching, too). When they're done, pictures can either be saved to Photos or emailed to granny or grandad.

Spawn Illuminati HD

This one is for all the hippies out there – by tapping and swiping, you control the creation of multicoloured psychedelic patterns on the iPad screen. There's even a public Flickr gallery (flickr.com/groups/spawn) where you can post your creations for the world to see.

Part 7

·························

Communicating

iPad email

How to set up and use email

Rather than email being something you do maybe twice a day, wedded to a desk, the iPad makes email available to you on the couch, in the kitchen, in bed... but unlike the experience of a netbook or laptop, the experience becomes effortless and comfortable. Like iPhones and the iPod Touch, the iPad comes with an email program known as Mail, which though elegant and easy to use, lacks some of the features that you might have come to expect from your desktop email application. What's more, the iPad's screen real estate makes webmail services, such as Gmail's, a viable alternative to the built-in Mail client.

Setting up email accounts

The iPad's Mail application and Settings panel come preconfigured to work with email accounts from Microsoft Exchange, AOL, Gmail, MobileMe and Yahoo! If you use one of these email providers, you may be used to logging in via a website (and indeed, it's perfectly possible to do this on the iPad, via Safari). However, it's generally faster and

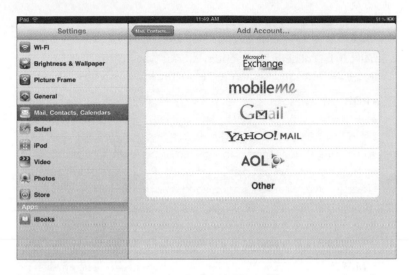

more convenient to use a dedicated mail program – such as Mail on the iPad.

To set up one of the aforementioned accounts, tap through from **Settings > Mail, Contacts, Calendars > Add Account...** (pictured above), choose your account provider from the list and enter your normal login details. Under **Description**, give your email account a label, for example "Personal" or "Work"; this has nothing to do with logging in with your email provider, so can be whatever you want and is your means of distinguishing between multiple email accounts within the iPad's Mail application.

You may be prompted to log in to your account on the web and enable either POP3 or IMAP access (see our jargon buster, overleaf). You can do this quickly and easily via Safari on your iPad, or using a computer.

Email jargon buster

Email can be collected and sent in various ways, the most common being POP, IMAP and Exchange. Here's the lowdown on each type:

• **POP** With a POP (or POP3) email account, messages can be sent and received via an email program, such as Mail on the iPad. Each time you check your mail, new messages are downloaded from your provider's mail server into your email program. It's a bit like a real-world postal service – and, indeed, POP stands for Post Office Protocol. When using a computer and mail program in this way, messages are usually deleted from the server as you download them. Though it is possible to leave copies "in the cloud", POP3 is really all about managing email with desktop mail applications.

• **IMAP** An IMAP account can also send and receive via an email program, but all the messages are based in the cloud, not on your computer. If you do use a mail program with IMAP set up, it downloads the email headers (from, to, subject, etc). Clicking on a message will download the full text of the message, but not delete it from the server. IMAP stands for Internet Message Access Protocol.

• **Exchange** Exchange is Microsoft's corporate system. If you use Outlook at work, it's likely that you're using an Exchange email account; and, assuming your administrator allows it, you can set up an Exchange account so that you can access it via the web, from a home computer using a mail program, or from your mobile, smartphone or iPad.

• **Web access** Most POP, IMAP and Exchange email providers also let you send and receive email via a website. Everything resides in the cloud, and you read and compose your mail from within a web browser. Gmail is designed for use via the web in this way.

Contacts and calendars too?

In the case of both Microsoft Exchange and MobileMe, you might well be prompted to set up contacts and calendars. If you do this, be aware that this setting will override any previous contact or calendar syncs that you have previously set up for your iPad within iTunes. Now your contacts and calendars will be "pushed" from the Exchange or MobileMe server online. To get the same results with Google contacts and calendars, you need to set up your account using the Microsoft Exchange option (see p.183).

Multiple alias addresses

If your email account has multiple alias addresses set up (with a MobileMe Account, for example, you can have up to five), and you want to be able to choose which appears in the "From" field when composing emails on the iPad, there is a cunning way to get this set up. When entering account details, include all the addresses (with a comma and a space between each) within the **Address** field. If the keyboard isn't showing a comma, tap the ⌨123 and then the ⌨ key to reveal it.

When configured, switch between addresses by tapping your default address in the **From** field to display a popover of all the available options. In some cases an initial tap might be necessary to separate out the **From** field from the **Cc** and **Bcc** fields.

From: mycandle@me.com

mycandle@me.com ✓

peter.buckley@uk.roughguid...

Setting up corporate Exchange email

Corporate-style Exchange email is fully compatible with the iPad, though only if the network administrator activates IMAP access on the server. If your office won't allow this, one workaround is to ask your Exchange administrator to allow you to sign up for the SyncYourMail service (pimmanager.divido.dk), which cleverly uses Exchange web access to map your email and other data onto the iPad's Mail application. It costs €40 a year.

Setting up other email accounts via iTunes

If you have a regular email account that you use with Mail, Outlook, Outlook Express or Entourage on your Mac or PC (an account from your broadband provider, for example), then it's simple to copy across your account details onto your iPad. This won't copy across the actual messages – just the details about your accounts so that you can begin sending and receiving on the iPad. To get things going, connect your iPad to your Mac or PC, select its icon in iTunes and choose the **Info** tab in the main panel. Scroll down, check the **Sync Mail Accounts** box and then also check the box for each account you want to copy across. Finally, press **Apply**.

Setting up other email accounts via the iPad

If you have an email account that you only access via the web, rather than with an email program, and it isn't

Push versus fetch

Traditionally, a computer or phone only receives new emails when its mail application contacts the relevant server and checks for new messages. On a computer, this happens automatically every few minutes – and whenever you click the **Check Mail** or **Send/Receive** button. This is referred to by Apple as a "fetch" setup.

By contrast, email accounts that support the "push" system feed messages to the iPad the moment they arrive on the server – which is usually just seconds after your correspondent clicks the Send button. The Yahoo!, Microsoft Exchange and MobileMe services are all examples that use the push system for emails, contacts and calendars.

To turn on push services for those accounts that support it, tap **Settings** > **Mail, Contacts, Calendars** > **Fetch New Data**. Here, you can also set up how frequently you would like accounts that use fetch to check in with the server to see if there are any new emails available. It's worth noting that the more frequently that emails and other data are fetched, the quicker your battery will run down. These settings also apply to other apps (such as some to-do list tools and instant messaging clients) that rely on Apple's push services to grab your up-to-date data from a server.

If you want the convenience of push email without switching accounts, one option is to set your existing account to forward all your mail to a free Yahoo! account, and set up both on the iPad. The Yahoo! account will alert you to new messages instantaneously, which will then appear in your regular account when you open Mail, allowing you to reply as normal. Ask your email provider whether they can activate forwarding for you.

☐ **Sync Mail Accounts**

Selected Mail accounts:

☑ myromancandle@me.com (MobileMe:myro...

Syncing Mail accounts syncs your account settings, but not your messages. To add accounts or make other changes, tap Settings then Mail, Contacts, Calendars on this iPad.

Other

Your bookmarks are being synced with your iPad over the air from MobileMe.
Over-the-air sync settings can be changed on your iPad.

☐ Sync notes

provided by AOL, Gmail, MobileMe or Yahoo!, then contact your provider to ask whether the account offers POP or IMAP access. If it does, get the details and set up the account on the iPad manually. You should be able to find a page on their website that spells out everything you need to know to set things up. You just need to plug in the account details yourself, being careful to type in everything exactly as your email provider directs you to.

To get started, tap **Settings > Mail, Contact, Calendars > Add Account… > Other** on the iPad. Next choose from **IMAP, POP** or **Exchange**. If you're not sure, try **POP**.

Next, fill in the details. If you're not sure and your email address is, say, **joebloggs@myisp.com**, the username may be **joebloggs** (or your full email address), the incoming server may be **mail.myisp.com** or **pop.myisp.com**; and your outgoing server may be **smtp.myisp.com**. Press **Save** when you're done.

Using the Mail application

Using email on the iPad works just as you'd expect. Tap
Mail on the Home Screen to kick-start the application and
then either hold the iPad in landscape mode to use Mail
in a split-screen column view (with your Inbox on the left)
or hold it in the portrait mode to see your messages full-
width with a button at the top of the screen which reveals
your Inbox or folders as a popover panel. Then…

• **Compose a message** Tap ✉ (If you have more than one
account set up, first select the account you want to use from the
list.) Alternatively, you can begin a message by tapping a name in
Contacts and then tapping the contact's email address.

• **View a message** Tap any email listed in your Inbox to view the
entire message. Double-tap, pinch and swipe to zoom in, zoom
out and scroll, respectively. If you often find that you have to
zoom in to read the text, try increasing the minimum text size
under **Settings > Mail**.

• **Move between messages** In landscape mode this is simply
done by selecting a different message in the left-hand column. In
portrait mode, however, where the Inbox/Folders column is not
always visible, use the ▲ and ▼ buttons at the top to move up
and down through your emails.

• **Move between accounts and folders** This is done by moving
"to the left", so to speak, in the Inbox/Folders area (the column
in landscape mode or popover panel in portrait mode). The left-
pointing arrow button at the top, above the search field displays
the name of the item one layer up in the hierarchy of folders and
accounts, with the latter farthest to the left.

Tip: Move to the top of long emails or scrolling lists by tapping the iPad's Status Bar at the top of the screen.

• **Open an attachment** You can open Word, Excel, PowerPoint, PDF and iWork files attached to emails. You can also view images and save them to Photos to be synced across to your computer. Tap the image in question and choose **Save Photo**.

• **Reply or forward** Open a message and tap ← at the top.

• **Deleting messages** You can delete individual messages when reading them by tapping the 🗑 icon at the top of the screen. You can also delete messages from the Inbox by swiping left or right over the message and then tapping **Delete**. Alternatively, to delete multiple messages, tap **Edit** and check each of the messages you want to trash. Then hit the **Delete** button.

• **Moving messages** The easiest way to move a message you are reading is to tap the 📁 button at the top of the screen in either landscape or portrait mode. To move one or more messages to a different folder, hit **Edit** at the top of the Inbox/Folders panel, check the messages and tap **Move**.

• **To attach a photo** You can't add an attachment to a message that you have already started directly from Mail, but you can **Paste** images that have already been copied using the **Copy** command in another application. To reveal the **Paste** command, tap and hold within the message you are composing. You can also create an email from an image in the iPad's Photos app (and many other third-party apps too): select an image, and tap

. Next tap **Email Photo** and type an accompanying message in the normal way. If you have multiple email accounts, the message will be sent from the default account, which you can select from the iPad's **Settings > Mail** panel.

• **Empty the Trash** Each email account offers a Trash folder alongside the Inbox, Drafts and Sent folders. When viewing the contents of the Trash, you can permanently delete individual items in the normal way. Alternatively, choose **Settings** from the Home Screen and select **Mail, Contacts, Calendars**, then choose an account, and tap **Advanced > Remove** and choose to have messages in the Trash automatically deleted after a day, a week, a month, or not at all.

Tip: As with Safari, tap and hold a link in an email to reveal the full destination address.

• **Create new contacts from an email** The iPad automatically recognizes phone numbers, as well as email and postal addresses when they appear in an email. Simply press and hold the relevant text to see the options to **Create a new contact**, **Add to an existing contact** or **Copy** to the clipboard. In the case of a postal address, you will also get the option to see the location in Google Maps.

Tweaking the settings

Once your email account is up and running on your iPad, scan through the Settings options to see what suits you. From the Home Screen, tap **Settings > Mail, Contacts, Calendars** and take a look at the available options. Here's a few things to consider:

• **Message preview** If you'd like to be able to see more of each message without clicking it, select **Preview** and increase the number of lines.

• **To/Cc** If you'd like to be able to see at a glance whether you were included in the To: or Cc: field of an email, toggle the **Show To/Cc Label** to the **On** position.

• **Sent mail** You may well find that messages sent from your iPad don't get transferred to the Sent folder on your Mac or PC. If this bothers you, as you'd like to have a complete archive of your mail on your computer, turn on **Always Bcc Myself**. The downside is that every message you send will pop up in your iPad Mail Inbox a few minutes later. The upside is that you'll get a copy of your sent messages next time you check your mail on your Mac or PC. You can copy these into your Sent folder manually, or set up a rule or filter to do it automatically.

• **Default account** If you have more than one email account set up on the iPad, you can choose one to be the default account. This will be used whenever you create messages from other applications – such as when you email a picture from within Photos. So choose the account that you're most likely to use in this way, which might not necessarily be the one you use the most.

• **Adding a signature** Even if you have a sign-off signature (name, contact details, etc) set up on your Mac or PC, it won't show up automatically when you use the same account from the iPad. To set up a mail signature for your iPad, tap **Signature** and then enter your sign-off details.

• **Show** Use the **Show** option to determine how many messages are displayed within your Mail Inbox… this is particularly useful if you are in denial about the amount of mail you have to get through!

• **Mail days** Microsoft Exchange users can also increase or decrease the number of email messages displayed on the iPad from an Exchange mail account. This can be done from the **Mail days to sync** option within the specific settings screen for the given Exchange account.

Email problems

You can receive but not send

If you're using an account from your Internet Service Provider, you might find that you can receive emails on the iPad but not send them. If you entered the details manually on the iPad, go back and check that you entered the outgoing (SMTP) mail server details correctly, and that your login details are right.

If that doesn't work, contact your ISP and ask for an outgoing server address that can be accessed from anywhere, or if they can recommend a "port" for mobile access. If they can, add this number, after a colon, onto the name of your outgoing mail server – which you'll find by tapping **Settings > Mail, Contacts, Calendars** and then choosing your account. If your server is smtp.myisp.com and the port number is 138, enter smtp.att.yahoo.com:138.

If you have more than one email account set up on your iPad, also try using an alternate outgoing mail server. To make sure that they are all available to be used by any given account, select that account, as above, and then tap **SMTP** and then toggle the other servers **On** within the **Other SMTP Servers** area of the panel.

You can't send or receive mail from an account

Sometimes, problems can arise when multiple devices (an iPad, iPhone and Mac or PC, say) are all trying to access the same mail account simultaneously. This is sometimes referred to as a "lock-out" issue. Apple's advice is to close your Mac or PC's email application when not using it or, alternatively, set your iPad to fetch emails less frequently, via the **Settings > Mail, Contacts, Calendars > Fetch New Data** screen.

There are messages missing

The most likely answer is that your POP3 email account downloaded them to your Mac or PC before your iPad had a chance to do so. Most email programs are set up to delete messages from the server once they've successfully downloaded them. However, it's easy to change this.

First, open your mail program and view the account settings. In most programs, look under the **Tools** menu. Click the relevant account and look for a "delete from server" option, which is usually buried under **Advanced**.

Choose to have your program delete the messages one week after downloading them. This way your iPad will have time to download each message before they get deleted.

Messages don't arrive unless I check for them

Unless you use an account that supports the "push" mail system, then you are relying on your iPad's "fetch" settings to retrieve emails for you from the server. To check that it

Beware the phishermen

"Phishing" is a cunning form of online scam in which someone pretends to be from your bank, ISP or other such company, and asks you to hand over your personal information either directly or via a webpage. The classic example is a scammer sending out a mass email claiming to be from a bank, with a link pointing to a webpage purportedly on a real bank's website. In fact, all the details are slightly incorrect (for example, the page might be at www.hsbc-banking.com instead of www.hsbc.com). But the recipient might not notice and assume the email is legitimate, following the instructions to "confirm" their online banking details on the fake site – in the process giving them to a criminal, who can then empty their account. The moral of the story is never to respond to emails – or instant messages – requesting private information, however legitimate the message might seem.

is configured the way you want it, tap your way through to **Settings > Mail, Contacts, Calendars > Fetch New Data**. Of course, your iPad will also need to have an available Internet connection (over either Wi-Fi or 3G) to check in with your email account provider.

I get a copy of all the messages I send

It could be that **Always Bcc Myself** is switched on under **Settings > Mail, Contacts, Calendars**. This feature does have its uses, but it can also be very annoying.

Rather use webmail?

These days, most email accounts offer some kind of webmail access, which is perfect for many users on a domestic Mac or PC, and will also suit many iPad users: if you know your Internet access is always on (touch wood), then there really is no need to use an email client as everything you need is always available online, via a web browser.

The iPad's email application, as we have seen, is a very nice piece of kit, but you really don't have to use it, especially if you only intend to use your iPad in the home, with an always-on Internet connection.

The two main advantages of sticking with webmail for the iPad are, firstly, that you will be using the same browser-based tools and setup that you are used to, and secondly, you won't be clogging up your iPad with a copy of an email archive which you will already have online, and perhaps even on a desktop or laptop machine that *does* run an email application. On the downside, when you're viewing your messages via the web, you may have to view adverts on the page and there's no guarantee the service will remain free forever.

At the time of writing there are many email choices out there that offer some kind of web access. Apple's MobileMe email service is a popular choice, but the "cloud" access is nowhere near as fast as the iPad's Mail application. Other popular choices come from Yahoo! and Microsoft, but whether their browser experience is good enough to compete with iPad Mail is really a matter of personal taste. The other major contender, which has already been mentioned in relation to the iPad's Mail application, is Google's Gmail.

Gmail on the iPad

Of all the webmail providers out there, Google have repeatedly shown themselves to be at the cutting edge of cloud-based services, and with each new Internet-capable device that comes along they have been swift to define their own place on that specific piece of kit.

Gmail users will not be disappointed. Making the most of the latest HTML5 technologies, Google have crafted a very nice two-pane email environment for the iPad that rivals the experience of the gadget's built-in Mail client. All you have to do to use it is point your iPad's Safari web browser to mail.google.com and log in to Gmail in the usual way… the Google servers detect that you are using an iPad and dish up the appropriate Gmail tool.

If you intend to use Gmail in Safari as your main email tool, then it's worth adding a special link, or "web-clip" to your iPad's Home Screen. To do this, open your Gmail account in Safari (as pictured) and then tap the **+** button at the top of the screen and choose **Add to Home Screen**.

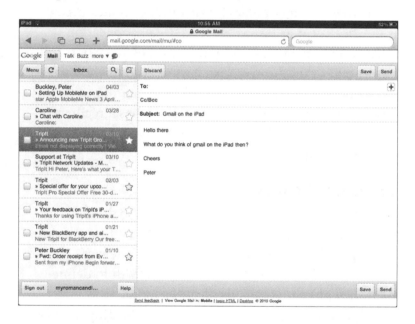

Other ways to connect

Calls, messages, chats and tweets

Perhaps the biggest disappointment of the first-generation iPad was the lack of a camera, which, had it been front-facing, would have enabled video calls over the Internet. It will surely come with a future incarnation of the device, but for now we have to make do with Internet audio calls. There are plenty of other ways to connect using the iPad as well, so whether your thing is Twitter, Facebook or instant messaging, you're sure to find an app that suits your needs. This chapter takes a quick look at a handful of apps that will help you get started.

Skype

Skype is what's known as a VoIP (Voice over Internet Protocol) client; in other words, it makes phone calls via the Internet as opposed to the traditional means used by the phone companies. Assuming you have broadband, you

BeejiveIM   Skype   IM+

can use the **Skype** app, with a Skype account, to make free audio calls to other Skype users, anywhere in the world. You can also pay to call regular landlines and mobile phones. This can be very useful if your home phone is often in use, effectively providing a second line without any standing charge. Potentially, it can also slash your phone bills, especially if you regularly call long-distance.

Skype also gives you a means of typing instant messages to other Skypers, in the same way that you can with other messaging clients, such as…

IM+

Most of the main networks and clients have been busily pushing out apps since the launch of the iPad. The **AIM** iPad app, for example, was among the very first apps to appear in the iPad section of the App Store when the device was launched, but it didn't work that hard to make the most of the iPad screen experience.

The IM+ app, on the other hand, is by far the best
instant messenger client currently available for the iPad.
It supports live chat with friends and buddies on Skype,
Facebook, Google Talk, Yahoo!, MSN, AIM, ICQ, MySpace
and Jabber, and can also keep you connected to Twitter.

Beejive

This great little client can be used to chat on AIM, iChat,
MobileMe, MSN, Yahoo!, MySpace, Google Talk, ICQ,
Jabber and Facebook. And thanks to push notifications,
your friends will see that they have received a message on
their iPad or iPhone, even when they don't have the app
running.

TweetDeck

Twitter was always going to be a big deal on the iPad, and there are many Twitter clients in the App Store to choose from. TweetDeck is a great choice: it works with multiple accounts, is very customizable, has excellent tools for locating tweets on a map, and has a very cool user interface.

Tip: For even more apps, look within **App Store > Categories > Social Networking.**

Setting up contacts and calendars

Via iTunes, via the iPad

You can, of course, enter all your contacts' details and calendar events manually on the iPad, though if you already have them stored in some other application, or perhaps online, it's far easier to synchronize them automatically, via either iTunes or a compatible "cloud" service.

Syncing via iTunes

Contacts

Open iTunes, connect your iPad and select its icon in the sidebar. You'll find the **Contacts** options under the **Info** tab. On a Mac you can choose to sync contacts with several different applications simultaneously, while on a PC you can only choose one:

☑ **Sync Address Book Contacts**

- **On a Mac** you'll find options to sync contacts with OS X's Address Book application, Yahoo! Address Book and Google Contacts.

- **On a Windows PC** you'll find options to sync contacts with Windows Address Book (via Outlook Express), Windows Vista Contacts, Microsoft Outlook 2003 or 2007, Google Contacts or Yahoo! Address Book.

Tip: If your contacts reside with an online service or application not supported by iTunes, use a service such as Plaxo (plaxo.com) to sync with one of the applications that iTunes does support.

Check the relevant sync option and choose whether you want to import all contacts or just particular groups. Once that's done, each time you connect your iPad, any new contact information added on the computer will be copied across to the iPad, and vice versa.

Tip: If your contacts currently exist only on a mobile phone, try connecting it to your computer via Bluetooth to move them to an application that will sync with the iPad.

Calendars

iPad calendars can be synchronized with your home computer using iTunes; again, the options are found under the **Info** tab:

- **On a Mac** you'll find an option to sync calendars with iCal.

- **On a Windows PC** you'll find an option for Microsoft Outlook.

Once syncing is set up, calendar data is merged between your computer and iPad, so deletions, additions or changes made in either place will be reflected in the other the next time you sync.

> **Tip:** If you have calendars on a phone that you want on your iPad, try to move them via Bluetooth onto your computer (so that you can get them into iCal, Entourage or Outlook).

Syncing with Entourage

Apple describe Entourage – the Mac version of Outlook – as being compatible with the iPad in terms of syncing contacts and calendars. But this isn't possible directly. In order to enable syncing between the iPad and Entourage, you first have to enable syncing between Entourage and the Apple Address Book and iCal. To do this, open Entourage and choose **Preferences** from the **Entourage** menu. Under **Sync Services**, check the boxes for **Contacts** and **Events**. If you can't find these options, you may need to update your software. Click **Check for Updates** in the Entourage **Help** menu.

Syncing with Microsoft Exchange

Most offices run their email, contacts and calendars via a system known as Microsoft Exchange Server. Individual workers access these various tools in the office, and a web address is made available to allow remote login from home or elsewhere. The iPad allows you to access Microsoft Exchange Servers directly (which is far neater than having to use your company's web services via Safari).

On the iPad tap **Settings > Mail, Contacts, Calendars > Add Account > Microsoft Exchange**, fill in your details and then turn on **Contacts** and **Calendars** when prompted.

If it doesn't work, or you are not sure how to fill in the fields, speak to your office network administrator. They might be able to supply you with a "configuration profile": this is a special file that you download from the web, or have sent to you via email; when opened on the iPad it does all the hard work for you and sets up your Exchange account ready for use.

> **Tip:** Your network administrator might also be able to offer you an LDAP Server Account. This won't sync your office contacts to the iPad, but it will allow you access to them when your iPad is online.

Syncing with Google Sync

If you want to sync your Google Contacts and Calendars, you can do this by using the **Add Account > Microsoft**

Contacts and calendars: fetching data

When you have your contacts and calendars synchronized via a server (as is the case with both Exchange and MobileMe), you can specify how often you want the iPad to query the server for up-to-date data… in other words, how often you want the iPad to "fetch" your data. You can also set up the servers to "push" data to the iPad automatically as changes become available. All these settings can be found within **Settings > Mail, Contacts, Calendars > Fetch New Data**.

Exchange option described above, rather than the **Add Account > Google Mail** option. For the full story, go to tinyurl.com/ipadgooglesync.

Syncing with MobileMe

If you use a MobileMe Account (see p.40), it is easily set up to sync your contacts and calendars on the iPad within **Settings > Mail, Contacts, Calendars > Add Account >**

MobileMe. Fill in the account details and turn on **Contacts** and **Calendars** when prompted.

> **Tip:** If you have already set up an Exchange or MobileMe mail account, open the account's info panel in **Settings > Mail, Contacts, Calendars** and check that **Contacts** and **Calendars** are turned on.

Subscribing to calendars

Another way to get calendars onto your iPad is to subscribe to them (they will need to be in either the CalDAV or iCalendar formats). Once on the iPad they will be read-only, so you won't be able to make any changes to them; still, it's useful for calendars of sporting events, national holidays and the like. To get started, tap **Settings > Mail, Contacts, Calendars > Add Account > Other**. Next tap either **Add CalDAV Account** or **Add Subscribed Calendar**. Enter the calendar server details and follow the prompts.

For a list of calendars that you might like to subscribe to, visit apple.com/downloads/macosx/calendars from your iPad; you'll find everything from the "Official F1 GP" racing calendar to the "Kazakhstan National and State Holidays" calendar. Tap the **Download** buttons for anything you fancy and you will be prompted to subscribe.

> **Tip:** It is also possible to subscribe to calendars published online by tapping a link that has been sent to you in an email.

The Contacts app

Your iPad's address book

Though perhaps not the most exciting thing to be found on the iPad, the Contacts app is arguably one of the most useful, especially if you find that you are using your iPad more and more like a digital Filofax. As well as names, numbers and addresses, the Contacts app has fields for all sorts of person-specific info, and because it keys in so well with the iPad's search feature (see p.72), it becomes an incredibly efficient means of retrieving contacts' details.

Using Contacts

Tap the Contacts app's icon on the Home Screen to get started. To browse the list, either flick up or down with your finger, or drag your finger over the alphabetic list on the left-hand edge to quickly navigate to a specific letter – useful if you have an extensive list of contacts. You can also return to the top of the list of contacts (or to the top of a long set of individual contact details) by tapping the iPad's Status Bar. To search for a contact, tap into the search field at the top and type in the first few characters of the name you're looking for. When you find the contact you want, tap once to view all their details, on the right-hand side.

From there, you can...

• **Email a contact** Tap a contact's email address to instantly be presented with a blank email message addressed to that contact from your default account.

• **Go to a website** Tap a contact's web address listing to have the iPad switch to Safari and take you straight to that webpage.

• **View a map** Tap a contact's address and the iPad will show you the location on Google Maps (assuming you have an Internet connection).

• **View Contact Groups** Tap the red **Groups** button at the top to view a specific set of contacts.

Tip: Groups cannot be created or edited on the iPad; they need to be set up on your computer before you sync.

• **Share a contact's details** Tap the **Share** button at the bottom to email someone a contact's details.

• **Copy any item** Tap and hold any field's entry and choose **Copy** from the options bubble that pops up.

Tip: By default the iPad sorts and displays your contacts by surname. To change this, tap **Settings > Mail, Contacts, Calendars** from the Home Screen and then scroll down to the **Contacts** options.

Adding and editing contacts

Tap the **+** button to create a new contact. To edit an existing contact – change their name or number, add an email address, or whatever – simply tap the relevant name in the main contacts list and hit **Edit**. Then...

• **Use the Add options** These are signified by a green ⊕ icon and are used to add a new number, address or other attribute.

• **Create new fields** If you can't see the relevant attribute, click **Add Field**. You'll then be offered everything from **Birthday** to a space for a **Nickname**.

• **Delete an item** To do this tap its red ⊖ icon. To delete the contact from your Contacts list entirely, scroll down to the bottom of the entry and tap the **Delete Contact** button.

• **Assign a picture to a contact** Tap add photo next to their name and then browse the photo albums on your iPad for a suitable snap. Once you've selected an image, you can pinch and drag to frame the snap just the way you want it. When you're done, click **Use**. To delete, edit or replace a photo associated with a contact, tap it and choose an option from the popover menu.

The Calendar app

Events and alerts

The iPad Calendar tool lets you view, add and edit events and appointments, and when set up using iTunes, syncs any changes you have made back to your computer whenever you connect. If your calendars have been set up with a service that supports "push" on the iPad (such as Microsoft Exchange or MobileMe), you'll find that any changes you make show up on your computer, and any other synced devices, almost instantly.

> **Tip:** Have you noticed that the Calendar icon on the iPad Home Screen always shows the correct date?

Using Calendar

You can view your schedule by month, week or day, or in a list (pictured overleaf), and it works in both portrait and landscape modes. From there on in, it really is pretty

self-explanatory: you tap an event to find out more details about it. You will also find options to...

- **View separate calendars** Tap **Calendars** to toggle different calendars (for Work, Home and Sport, say) on and off. When you create a new event you can choose which of your calendars you want to add it to.

- **Search for events** Tap into the search field at the top and type. You can also search from the iPad's Search Screen.

- **Add a new event** Tap **+** (bottom-right), enter whatever data you like, and tap **Done**. To edit or delete an existing event, tap the relevant entry and use the **Edit** button or **Trash** icon.

- **Delete an event** Tap the event, then **Edit**, and scroll down to tap the **Delete Event** button at the bottom.

Calendar alerts

The iPad also offers reminder alerts, which will pop up on the iPad's screen and make an annoying beeping sound (annoying enough not to be ignored anyway), meaning that you'll never have an excuse for tardiness again. You can set an alert to remind you of an impending event either as it happens or a certain number of minutes, hours or days beforehand. And you can set up multiple alerts for the same event. Look for the option when either creating or editing events.

If you'd like to have these alerts appear onscreen, but without the beep, tap **Settings > General > Sounds** and turn off the **Calendar Alerts** switch.

> **Tip:** For organizing and viewing busy school or college timetables and calendars, try the excellent **iStudiez** (there's both a "Lite" and "Pro" version available in the App Store).

Time Zone Support

Tap **Settings > Mail, Contacts, Calendars** and scroll down to find more Calendar-specific settings, including **Time Zone Support**, which controls whether the iPad displays events within the Calendar app for the time zone that the iPad's clock is set to (**Settings > General > Date & Time**) or for a Calendar app specific setting. If you're heading overseas for business meetings, it is essential that you get your head around how this works.

To-do lists

One thing the iPad Calendar tool doesn't currently support is to-do lists, such as those composed in iCal or Mail. There are, however, loads of great to-do list and task apps in the App Store that will help you out:

• **Remember The Milk** Arguably the best task-organizing sync service out there right now.

• **Things for iPad** A very clean-looking app with a really nice Projects area for bundling tasks.

• **Toodledo – To Do List** Another service that syncs your tasks to the cloud; nice split-screen interface.

What, no clock!

Well, actually yes, the iPad does have a clock, in so far as it displays the time at the top of the screen (you can change the time either manually or by specifying a time zone within **Settings > General > Date & Time**). What it lacks is specific alarm, timer and stopwatch functions, as well as any fancy analogue displays. Thankfully there are a plethora of apps available that can help you plug these gaps. Take a look in the App Store, or try one of these:

• **FlipTime XL** Great flip clock and calendar display app.

• **Alarm! HD** Digital-clock-style nightstand alarm tool.

• **Gourmet Egg Timer** For the perfect boiled egg, this app takes into account altitude, egg size and how soft you like your yolk.

Part 9

....

The World Wide Web

Safari

The iPad's web browser

The iPad comes with a version of the Safari web browser. Anyone who has ever used Safari on the iPhone or iPod Touch will feel very at home, while the extra screen size and speedy processing power of the iPad take things to another level. It can't do everything – Flash (a technology used for online video and animation) doesn't display – but Safari does conspire with the hardware to create one of the most impressive and compelling web browser experiences ever produced.

The basics

Make sure you have either a Wi-Fi or cellular data signal (3G, EDGE or GPRS), as discussed in the Connecting chapter, and then tap **Safari** on the Home Screen. Then...

• **Enter an address** Tap into the address field at the top of the screen; tap ⊗ to clear the current address and start typing. Note the ".com" key for quickly completing addresses. Then tap **Go**.

> **Tip:** If you tap and hold the ".com" key, other common web address suffixes appear: ".net", ".org", etc.

• **Search Google** Tap in the Google field at the top of the screen and start typing. When you're finished, hit **Google**. If you want to switch from Google to Yahoo! searching, look within **Settings > Safari > Search Engine**. Of course, you can also visit any search engine manually and use it in the normal way. For more search tips, see p.204.

• **Reload/refresh** If a page hasn't loaded properly, or you want to make sure you're viewing the latest version, click ↻.

• **To follow a link** Tap once. If you did it by accident, press ◀.

> **Tip:** You can see the full URL of any link on a page by tapping and holding the relevant text or image.

• **Send an address to a friend** When viewing a page, click the ✚ and then tap **Mail Link to this Page**. A new email will appear with the link in the body and the page's title in the subject line.

• **Scroll** You can use your fingers to scroll up, down or sideways in Safari on the iPad. One finger scrolls the entire page, two fingers will scroll within a specific frame of a webpage.

> **Tip:** Having scrolled down a long page, quickly get back to the top by tapping the clock display on the iPad's Status Bar at the top.

• **Zoom** Double-tap on any part of a page – a column, headline or picture, say – to zoom in or zoom back out. Alternatively, "pinch out" with your finger and thumb (or any two digits of your choice). Once zoomed, scroll around the page with one finger.

History and cache

Like most browsers, Safari on the iPad stores a list of all the websites you visit. These allow the iPad to offer suggestions when you're typing an address but can also be browsed – useful if you need to find a site for the second time but can't remember its address. To browse your history, look at the top of your Bookmarks list, accessible at any time via the 𝄞 icon. To clear your history, look for the option in **Settings > Safari.**

Unfortunately, despite storing your history, Safari doesn't "cache" (temporarily save) each page you visit in any useful way. This is a shame, as it means you can't quickly visit a bunch of pages for browsing when you're offline. It also explains why using the ◄ button is slower on the iPad than on a computer – when you click ◄, you download the page in question afresh rather than returning to a cached version.

Multiple pages

Just like a browser on a Mac or PC, Safari on the iPad can handle multiple pages at once. These are especially useful when you're struggling with a slow connection, and you don't want to close a page that you may want to come back to later.

- **Open a new blank page** Tap ⬒, then **New Page**.
- **Switch between pages** Tap ⬒ and then the page you want.
- **Close a page** Tap ⬒ and then ⊗ on a page's corner.

Tip: To open a web link into a new page tap and hold the link; then choose **Open in New Page** from the option bubble.

Webpage display problems

If a webpage looks weird on screen – bad spacing, images overlapping, etc – there are two likely causes. First, it could be that the page isn't properly "web compliant". That is, it looked okay on the browser the designer tested it on (Internet Explorer, for example), but not on other browsers (such as Safari on the iPad).

Second, it could be that the page includes elements based on technologies that the iPad doesn't yet handle, such as Adobe Flash. This is especially likely to be the problem if there's a gap in an otherwise normal page, though sometimes Safari closes such gaps where there should be Flash, which can play havoc with the page's intended layout.

If a webpage looks okay, but different from the version you're used to seeing on your Mac or PC, it could be that the website in question has been set up to detect your browser and automatically offer you a small-screen version.

Bookmarks

A bookmark is basically a saved link to a web address that you might want to come back to or use frequently. Bookmarks, like web-clips placed on the Home Screen, are always handy, and make the browsing experience quick and easy. They can also be set up to sync back to your Mac or PC automatically, so that you have them there too.

The basics

To bookmark a page on the iPad, click **+** when viewing the page and choose **Add Bookmark**. Use the upper field to

name your bookmark and the lower field to choose a folder
to keep it in (see below). To retrieve a bookmark, tap ▢,
browse and then click the relevant entry. It's also possible
to edit and organize your bookmarks and folders:

- **To create a bookmarks folder** Tap **Edit > New Folder** to add
a folder to the currently viewed list.

- **To delete a bookmark or folder** Tap **Edit**, followed by the
relevant ⊖ icon. Hit **Delete** to confirm.

- **To edit a bookmark or folder** Tap **Edit**, then hit the relevant
entry and type into the name and URL fields. From here you can
also create new folders and delete bookmarks.

- **To move a bookmark or folder** Tap **Edit** and slide it up or
down using the ≡ icon. Alternatively, tap **Edit**, then the item
you want to move, and then use the lower field to browse for the
folder you want to use.

> **Tip:** Bookmarks (and folders) placed in the **Bookmarks Bar** folder
> will appear as a strip below the address field in Safari when you tap
> into it. To make it permanently visible, visit **Settings > Safari**.

Importing bookmarks from your Mac or PC

iTunes lets you quickly transfer bookmarks from a Mac or PC to your iPad. Just connect your iPad and click its icon in iTunes. Under the **Info** tab, check the relevant box under **Other**. The bookmarks will move across to the iPad, though they can be easy to miss: if you use Safari on your Mac or PC, you'll find them within two folders labelled **Bookmarks Menu** and **Bookmarks Toolbar**.

Likewise, bookmarks from the iPad will appear back in your browser. In Safari, you won't find them in the **Bookmarks** menu, however: you'll have to click **Show All Bookmarks** or the 𝄢 icon. At the time of writing, iTunes will only sync bookmarks from Safari (Mac and PC) or Internet Explorer (PC), so if you use, say, Firefox or Chrome on your computer, you will first need to sync bookmarks to Safari to get them onto your iPad.

> **Tip:** Use the free Xmarks service (xmarks.com) to sync other browsers' bookmarks to Safari, to in turn get them onto the iPad.

Forms and AutoFill

You can set Safari on the iPad to remember the names and passwords that you use frequently on websites, though if you do, there is a risk that someone else could use those credentials on a website if they got hold of your iPad. You can turn the feature on or off within **Settings >**

Safari > AutoFill – look for the option to turn on **Names & Passwords**. If you do enable it, also consider setting a four-digit security code to unlock the iPad's Lock Screen, as an extra level of security. This is found within **Settings > General > Passcode Lock**.

AutoFill can also help you when filling out address fields on webpages, though you will need to tell the iPad which contact details to use for this. First enable AutoFill, as already described, and then turn on **Use Contact Info**, choose **My Info** and select your contact entry from your iPad's **Contacts** list.

If at any time you wish to remove all the saved passwords and usernames on your iPad, tap **Clear All**.

Safari settings

You'll find various browsing preferences under **Settings > Safari**. Here you can empty your cache and history (useful if Safari keeps crashing, or you want to hide your tracks), play with security settings (make sure that the **Fraud Warning** option is switched on), choose a search engine, turn the **Bookmarks Bar** on and off, and also access options for the following:

- **JavaScript** This is a ubiquitous way to add extra functions to websites and is best left on.

- **Cookies** These are files that websites save on your iPad to enable content and preferences tailored for you... for example, specific recommendations on a shopping site.

• **Pop-up blocker** stops pop-up pages (mainly ads) from opening.

• **Databases** Some advanced browser-based applications (such as those employed by Google) will store application information on the iPad in the form of a "database"; these are sometimes also referred to as "super cookies", and allow you to use such applications within a browser when offline. If you are having problems with specific sites within Safari, you may well find that deleting any databases they use can help.

More browsing tips

Searching for text on a page

One very useful tool currently missing in the iPad version of Safari is the ability to search for text within a page. This is especially annoying when you follow a link in Google and end up on a very long page with no idea where your search term appears.

A workaround for this is to get into the habit, when searching the web, of visiting Google's "cached" (saved and indexed) version of a webpage rather than the "live" version. You'll find a link for this option next to each of the results when you search Google. Click "Cached" and see a version of the target page that's got each of your search terms highlighted in a different colour throughout – almost as good as being able to click **Find**.

Viewing online PDFs and Word documents

The iPad can view Word, Excel and PDF documents on the web. Once opened, scroll down to read subsequent pages, and double-tap to zoom in just as you would with a regular webpage.

Unfortunately, that's all you can do, as there are no options to then save the PDF files to your iPad. You could, however, create a bookmark so that you can quickly return to the file again, assuming you are online, or use a dedicated PDF reader app (see p.118) that can save a copy of the file on the iPad for you.

iPad Googling tips

The Google search field at the top of each Safari page on the iPad is an incredibly useful tool and as you start to type, its dynamic popover list of suggested searches makes it even more so. But you can make it work even harder.

Given that your connection speed may be low when out and about, it makes sense to hone your search skills for use on the iPad. All the following tricks work on a PC or Mac, too. Typing the text in red will yield the following search results:

Basic searches

william lawes > the terms "william" and "lawes"

"william lawes" > the phrase "william lawes"

william OR lawes > either "william" or "lawes" or both

william -lawes > "william" but not "lawes"

All these commands can be mixed and doubled up. Hence:

"william lawes" OR "will lawes" -composer > either version of the name but not the word "composer"

Synonyms

~mac > "mac" and related words, such as "Apple" and "Macintosh"

Definitions

define:calabash > definitions from various sources for the word "calabash". You can also get definitions of a search term by clicking the **definitions** link at the right-hand end of the top blue strip on the results page.

Flexible phrases

"william * lawes" > "william john lawes", etc, as well as just "william lawes"

Search within a specific site

site:bbc.co.uk "jimmy white" > pages containing Jimmy White's name within the BBC website. This is often far more effective than using a site's internal search.

Search web addresses

"arms exports" inurl:gov > the phrase "arms exports" in the webpages with the term gov in the address (i.e. government websites)

Search page titles

train bristol intitle:timetable > pages with "timetable" in their titles, and "train" and "bristol" anywhere in the page

Number and price ranges

1972..1975 "snooker champions" > the term "snooker champions" and any number (or date) in the range 1972–1975

$15..$30 "snooker cue" > the term "snooker cue" and any price in the range $15–30

Search specific file types

filetype:pdf climate change statistics > would find PDF documents (likely to be more "serious" reports than webpages) containing the terms "climate", "change" and "statistics"

Webpages specially optimized for the iPad

Though the iPad can handle almost all webpages, and most look absolutely great, some are specially designed to work perfectly on the iPad screen – even mimicking the visual language of columns and buttons found in iPad apps. At the time of writing, the best example is Google's Gmail interface (for more, see the iPad email chapter).

Many such sites use the latest HTML5 technologies to create their look – a technology that Apple is championing as part of their much-hyped anti-Flash policy.

For a list of other websites built using HTML5 standards, visit apple.com/ipad/ready-for-ipad.

Other browsers

There are several alternative browsers available in the iPad App Store, but none that offers all the features and integration of Safari. Browse or search the **Utilities** and **Productivity** categories to see what's available, or try one of these:

• **SafeBrowse for iPad** A no-frills affair that offers completely private browsing sessions: no history, cache, cookies etc.

• **Tabbed Browser** Until it becomes a feature of Safari (as it surely will at some point), this is the app to download for a tabbed browsing fix.

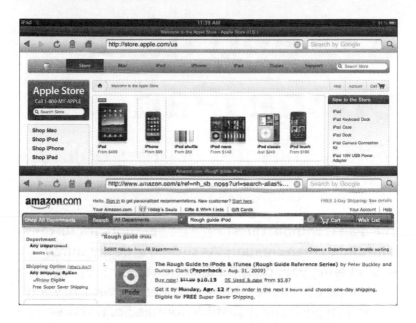

- **Duo Browser** One of several browsers in the Store that give you the functionality to browse two sites simultaneously on the same screen (pictured here).

- **Split Screen** This app also gives you two browsing panels, but with the one on the left in the form of a narrow column, not unlike the sidebar feature of Firefox on the Mac and PC.

- **Offline Pages** Very handy app for downloading and saving entire webpages so that you can read them offline without an Internet connection.

- **Opera Mini** Tabbed browsing, password tools and the quick access "Speed Dial" feature have all made Opera Mini a hit on the iPhone and iPod Touch. It's worth trying out on the iPad too.

RSS and news on the iPad

Making the most of news online

The iPad is without question a device more useful for consuming than creating. As such, it's ideally suited to delivering your daily fix of current affairs, or any other kind of news for that matter, wherever you want it, and in a perfectly digestible format. So, whether you read in bed, on the train, on the couch, or at the breakfast table, the iPad feels like a very comfortable replacement for a newspaper, magazine or periodical.

RSS

RSS – Really Simple Syndication – allows you to view "feeds" or "newsfeeds" from blogs, news services and other websites. Each feed consists of headlines and summaries of new or updated articles. If you see something you think you'd like to read, click on the headline to view the full story. One benefit of RSS is that it saves you regularly visiting your favourite sites to check for new content: if something's been added or changed, you'll always know about it. But the real beauty of the system is that you can use a tool called an aggregator or feed reader to combine the feeds from all your favourite sites. It's almost like having your own personalized magazine or newspaper.

At the time of writing, arguably the best web-based aggregator is Google Reader, which can be accessed via Safari. To get started, simply sign in using the same credentials you use for other Google services and start adding feeds:

- **Google Reader** reader.google.com

The alternative on the iPad is to download a dedicated RSS feed app, such as **Feeddler** (pictured here) or **NewsRack**. Search for them in the iTunes App Store, or visit their websites to find out more:

- **Feeddler** chebinliu.com

- **NewsRack** omz-software.de

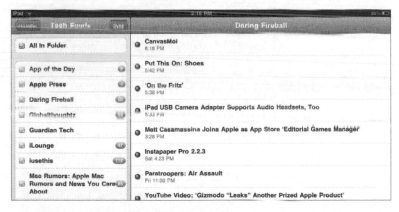

Also worth investigating is the free Instapaper service, which lets you save webpages and articles to read later. The **Instapaper** app has a really easy-on-the-eye stripped-back feel; many RSS services (including NetNewsWire) integrate with it, as does Twitter, so you can have all your reading matter and stories with you, and available offline (assuming you remember to sync your app and Instapaper account before you disconnect from the Internet).

• **Instapaper** instapaper.com

News apps

Many of the major news and magazine publishers are battling to define their place on the iPad, and within the the new digital marketplace as a whole. Some have opted to make their applications free, but with advertising support; some others are looking to get users to pay a subscription;

while others will charge a one-time fee for users to download their app.

The real question here is not whether you want to pay for your news (there are still a thousand places online where the latest stories can be harvested for free), but more whether you are prepared to pay for a particular stance, attitude or editorial voice... which is what we do in the real world when we choose to hand over cash for a print newspaper.

All the major news voices are represented on the iPad, and there is even a **News** category in the App Store to help find what you are looking for. From a useability perspective, here are a couple of recommendations:

• **BBC News** This app has a really nice split-screen view in both landscape and portrait modes, complete with a handy news-ticker that dishes up the latest headlines.

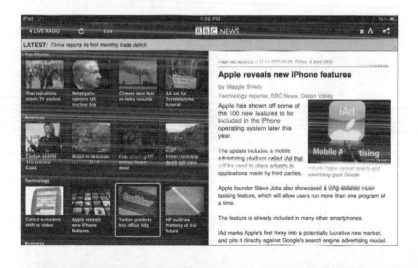

• **The Wall Street Journal** Register for free to see the latest news presented in a beautiful format that successfully mimics the look of the print version. For full access to the Business, Markets and Opinion sections you need to buy a subscription.

• **USA Today** A really nice interface with an easy-to-navigate layout. Scrolling from page to page of long articles is particularly well handled.

• **NYT Editors' Choice** Though a little heavy on the in-app advertising, navigation is good and there are dedicated sections for News, Business, Technology, Opinion and Features.

• **Zinio** This app is a one-stop shop for magazines. There are hundreds on offer, plenty of free samples, and you can choose to purchase either single issues or annual subscriptions. There's a handy calendar view that shows you which issues you'll be getting to read each month.

Staying safe online

How to avoid hackers and scammers

The Internet may be the greatest wonder of the modern world, but it does come with certain downsides. Increased access to information is great, but not if the information other people are accessing is yours – and private. Of course, there are threats to privacy and security in the real world, but on the Internet things are different, not least because your private data might be compromised without you even knowing about it. And though Apple products are generally very secure, it's still worth remembering a few golden rules.

Protect yourself

If you want to keep your iPad, your files, and your private data safe, read the next couple of pages and make sure that you check all the boxes.

Keep your system up to date

Many security breaches involve a programmer taking advantage of a security flaw in your software. So it's critical to keep your iPad's software up to speed with the latest firmware updates. You should be prompted automatically when updates are available, but to check for yourself, connect your iPad to iTunes. Next select your iPad in the iTunes sidebar and then under the **Summary** tab, click **Check for Updates**.

Don't run dodgy software

Apple work hard to ensure that all the software that they make available in the App Store will be "clean" of viruses and other dangers. However, if you're offered any alternative routes to getting software onto your iPad, such as jailbreaking, steer clear… it's not worth the risk.

Hide behind a firewall

A firewall serves to prevent anyone from being able to find your computer, iPad or other devices on the Internet, let alone invade it. If you use a wireless router at home, then you may well find that it has its own firewall. Make sure it's enabled and your iPad will be undetectable from the Internet when connected via Wi-Fi at home.

Enable wireless security

Also, be sure to implement a few basic security measures to secure your domestic Wi-Fi network. First, add a WPA or

WPA2 password (the older WEP standard just doesn't cut it these days) to make sure your connection is only used by the people you want to use it. Next, make sure you set a username and password for accessing your router settings (and make sure it's different to your Wi-Fi network's WPA password).

Don't respond to spam

Those "get paid to surf", "stock tips", "recruit new members", "clear your credit rating" and various network-marketing schemes are always too good to be true.

> **Tip:** Also beware of "phishermen" trying to snag your bank details and passwords. For more, see p.171.

Be careful of "adult" sites

It is often said that the majority of online scams involve porn sites – the scammers believing, probably correctly, that the victims will be too embarrassed to report the problem. If you do ever use an adult site, never pass over credit card details unless you're prepared to get stung. And, whatever you do, don't download any software they offer.

Security on the road

Next, here's a few golden rules to help keep your iPad's data safe and secure away from home, and particularly when connected to public Wi-Fi networks.

Always use a screen lock

Always use a password-protected screen lock so that, should your machine be lost or stolen, its data will be inaccessible. Look in **Settings** > **General** > **Passcode Lock**. Also turn on the **Erase Data** function so that all your iPad's content is wiped after ten failed passcode attempts.

Avoid using banking sites out and about

If you use Wi-Fi hotspots, avoid accessing your bank accounts and any other sensitive material, as public networks are notorious for so-called "snoop" or "sidejacking" attacks, where data is intercepted by other machines using the same network. Where possible limit your activities to browsing that isn't security-sensitive. And always try to shield your keystrokes when entering passwords, just as you would with your PIN at an ATM.

MobileMe... Find My iPad

If you have an Apple MobileMe Account you can use the "Find My iPad" feature to remotely track the location of your iPad, add a four-digit passcode and even wipe all its content remotely. To enable the feature, go to **Settings > Mail, Contacts, Calendars > MobileMe > Find My iPad**.

Passwords

You probably have a plethora of passwords and user IDs for the sites you frequently visit. Though obvious, there are a few basic ground rules worth reiterating here to make sure that your online identity remains secure – from online criminals, but also from members of your household who might inadvertently use your logins.

In terms of Safari, it's worth treating your iPad just as you would a public machine and making sure that it doesn't remember your passwords and login details by default as you browse (**Settings > Safari > AutoFill**). The same goes for any apps that require passwords.

- **Make them "strong"** It really should go without saying that you shouldn't use the word "password" as a password. Neither should you opt for pets' or family members' names. Instead, go for something with both letters and numbers, upper and lower case, and preferably that makes no sense at all.

- **Use multiple passwords** It's a good idea to create separate passwords for different logins on different sites. That way, if the password you use on one site is compromised, there is no danger that it can be used for any other sites. If this sounds like way too much to have to remember, come up with a secret formula – perhaps using the same basic root for all your passwords and then adding the initials of a given website's name.

• **Change them regularly** Again, this might sound like time that could be spent doing something less boring instead, but get into the habit of refreshing your passwords on a regular basis.

Secure your connections

Whenever entering sensitive data (passwords, usernames and the like) into a webpage, make sure that the address at the top of the browser begins "https://" rather than simply "http://". The "s" signifies a secure connection that uses the so-called SSL (Secure Sockets Layer) or newer TLS (Transport Layer Security) protocols. If you are at all unsure about the security provided by a specific online site or service, drop them a line and ask for some clarity. If they don't give you a satisfactory response, use a different service.

Password managers

Another option for managing the myriad passwords you have now collected is a password manager. This is basically a piece of software that stores all your login details within an encrypted database on your iPad, or computer, ready for you to call upon when visiting sites.

As already mentioned, Safari has the AutoFill feature (found in **Settings > Safari**), though when enabled, it gives everyone who uses your iPad access to your logins.

There are also third-party password managers out there for the iPad, which sell themselves on the premise that their encryption is stronger than that offered by Safari and that they can sync logins and passwords across multiple devices. The best of the bunch is **1Password Pro** (pictured here), though it does still have its limitations. The main problem is that it doesn't integrate with Safari on the iPad, so to take advantage of its login tools, you need to browse the sites in question using the integrated browser – only really worth doing for particularly sensitive sites. Find out more at:

• **1Password Pro** agilewebsolutions.com

Restrictions

Finally, a note on the iPad's parental control features, which can be employed to stop users accessing Safari, YouTube, the iTunes and App Stores, plus location services.

You can also prevent "in-app" purchases and set content-specific age limits for music, movies, TV shows and apps. You'll find the various options in **Settings > General > Restrictions**, where you also get to set a passcode to gain access to the quarantined activities and features.

Settings		General	Restrictions	
Wi-Fi	Hoth			
Notifications	On		**Disable Restrictions**	
Brightness & Wallpaper		Allow:		
Picture Frame		Safari		ON
General		YouTube		ON
Mail, Contacts, Calendars		iTunes		ON
Safari		Installing Apps		ON
iPod		Location		ON
Video		Allowed Content:		
Photos		In-App Purchases		ON
Store		Ratings For	United States >	
Apps		Music & Podcasts	Explicit >	
AirVideoFree		Movies	All >	
BBC News		TV Shows	All >	
Brushes		Apps	All >	
Classics				

Maps
Search and directions

The Maps app on the iPad (tap the icon on the Home Screen to get started) takes you into the world of Google Maps, where you can quickly find locations, get directions and view satellite photos. You can zoom and scroll around the maps in the same way you would with webpages in Safari, the difference being that, because you're using your own digits to drag and pinch, the whole experience feels much more natural. It works okay over EDGE and GPRS, though it's far quicker using 3G, and even better with Wi-Fi.

> **Tip:** To zoom in either double-tap one finger or spread two apart; to zoom out again, either pinch or tap once with two digits.

Searching for yourself

The 3G-capable iPad can accurately determine your current location by using a combination of data from its GPS (Global Positioning System) chip, a connected cellular network and also from a connected Wi-Fi network. The Wi-Fi-only iPad, on the other hand, has only got Wi-Fi to

go on, so it needs to be connected to a network to be able
to determine your location.

Tip: Hold the iPad flat and tap the target icon for a second time; the
device's compass springs to life, allowing you to view the map in
relation to the points of the compass.

Searching for a location

Tap the Search box and type a city, town or region, place of
interest, or a ZIP or post code. (As you type, the iPad will
try to predict the location based on previous map searches
and address entries in your Contacts list.) You can also try
to find a business in the area you are viewing by entering
either the name of the business or something more general
– such as "camera", "hotel", or "pizza". Note, however, that
the results, which are pulled from Google Local, won't be
anything like comprehensive.

Search results appear as a little red pin. If a multitude of pins appears, tap on each of the listings in the popover menu (pictured) to identify them on the map. Tap the pin's blue i icon for further options, such as adding the location as a bookmark or contact address, emailing a link to the location or getting directions to or from that location.

> **Tip:** In some areas you will also see a little red icon on a pin's name bubble. Tap this to scroll around in Google's Street View. When you're finished, tap the screen once to show the **Done** button.

Dropping pins

You can also drop a pin manually at any time by tapping the curl of the map, bottom-right, and then **Drop Pin**. This can be handy to keep your bearings when sliding around a map. To change the position of a pin, tap and hold it and then drag. To delete the pin, add it as a bookmark, add it to a contact, email the location or get directions, tap the pin and then the i icon. Your lists of bookmarks and recently viewed locations can be viewed by tapping the ⌂ icon.

Satellite and Terrain views

Tapping the page curl reveals options to view **Satellite** images (they're not live, unfortunately… maybe one day), a very impressive **Terrain** view (check out the Himalayas) and a **Hybrid** view that adds roads and labels from the **Classic** view to a satellite image.

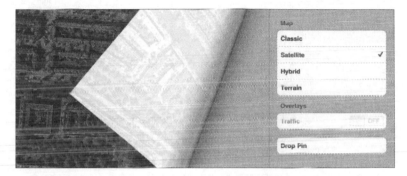

Directions

To view directions between two locations, tap **Directions** at the top of the screen and enter start and end points, either by typing search terms or by tapping ⌂ to browse for bookmarks, addresses from your Contacts and recently viewed items. The route is automatically refreshed as you change the contents of the start or end point fields. Use the three icons on the lower panel to choose between directions for driving, walking or taking the bus.

Tip: Where a search term that yielded multiple results has been used as an end point, tap the ☰ icon to quickly switch between the different pins, and in turn, refresh the route.

Once a journey is displaying, you can go through it one step at a time by tapping **Start** and using the arrow buttons to jump forward and back one stage. Alternatively, tap ▤ to view all the stages as a series of text instructions. Tap any entry in the list to see a map of that part of the journey.

Tip: For your return journey, reverse the directions given by your iPad by tapping the ↺ button between the start and end point fields.

Though not available at the time of writing, Apple are intending to incorporate turn-by-turn navigation (just like a sat-nav that you might find in a car) to their Maps app very soon, though you are obviously going to need a 3G-capable iPad to get the feature to work. You could alternatively download one of the dedicated sat-nav apps already available in the App Store. Several of the big brands (including TomTom) have apps available, though whether they can maintain their high prices alongside the Google Maps offering remains to be seen.

Traffic conditions

In areas where the service is available, your route will display colour-coded information about traffic conditions. The approximate driving time at the top of the iPad screen will change to take account of the expected traffic and the roads will change colour:

- **Grey** No data currently available

- **Red** Traffic moving at less than 25 miles per hour

- **Yellow** Traffic moving at 25–50 miles per hour

- **Green** Traffic moving at more than 50 miles per hour

If you don't see any change in colour, you may need to zoom out a little. This action will also automatically refresh the traffic speed data. To hide the traffic information (perhaps you like surprises), tap the map curl and toggle the **Traffic** button off.

Maps, apps and navigation

The App Store has its own category dedicated to Navigation, where you'll find everything from multi-functional compass applications (**Compass XL**) to plane and ship location tools (**Plane Finder HD** and **Ship Finder HD**). Also search "maps" to unearth some interesting cartographic relics (**HistoryMaps**) as well as some very impressive reference tools (**National Geographic World Atlas HD**). And a few more...

- **Yellow Pages** A really nicely presented app for locating local businesses and amenities. A very useful alternative to the search results that the iPad's Maps app throws up.

- **Flightwise Chart Explorer** Aviation maps with satellite and weather overlays.

- **MapTap** Useful tool for downloading maps to be used offline (which you will need to do before you head out of the door if you have a Wi-Fi-only iPad). You can choose to use maps from either Open Street Map, Open Cycle Map or CloudMade.

- **Transit Maps** Use this app to locate, download and store transit maps from around the world that you can then use offline.

- **iTopoMaps** Beautifully rendered maps for hiking and climbing in the US. Maps can be saved to use offline, and work with the iPad's location services, allowing you to pinpoint where you are.

- **iOS Maps** A similar app to the above, but for the UK, courtesy of Ordnance Survey.

- **Point Inside** For those who want to combine shopping and gadgets, this app offers navigation within malls across the US.

iWork apps and other tools

A roundup of productivity apps

Much of this book has looked at the iPad as a device for consuming content – watching video, listening to music, reading books, etc. The iPad is well suited to such tasks, but it also has a few things to contribute to the way we get things done. This chapter takes a quick look at some of the available apps for working with words, numbers, presentations, and the like. And while the iPad sometimes struggles to replicate the large-screen experience of many desktop applications, there are some handy tools up for grabs that might be just enough to convince you to leave your laptop at home next time you head out the door.

The first thing that most people ask when thinking of the iPad as a possible "work" machine is whether it can deal with Microsoft Office documents, or perhaps even run the Office software. At the time of writing Microsoft have not announced any plans to launch their Office suite for the iPad; Apple have, however, taken the opportunity to completely redesign theirs. The iWork suite has existed on Macs since 2005, but has never had the take-up of Microsoft Office. Reinvented for the iPad, iWork now looks like it is going to have its moment of glory. It consists of three separately available apps (which cost $9.99 each), **Pages** (pictured here), **Numbers** and **Keynote**, each of which is dealt with below and can respectively open and edit documents from Microsoft's Word, Excel and PowerPoint.

Tip: If you're a Google Docs user, you'll find it works really well on the iPad in Safari; simply visit docs.google.com.

File sharing with apps

Many apps, including the three members of the iWork suite, utilize the File Sharing feature of iTunes as a means of transferring files back and forth between the iPad and your computer. If a particular app supports the feature, it will appear within the **File Sharing** panel in the lower area of the **Apps** tab in iTunes when your iPad is connected. From there you can drag files in (or use the **Add** button to browse for files) and drag files out (or use the **Save to** button to browse for a location to save to).

If you would rather share files between your iPad and computer over Wi-Fi, use an app such as **Air Sharing HD**, and for sharing via the web, **Dropbox** or **MobileMe** (see p.40).

Working with words

• **Pages** This app is the iWork word-processing and layout tool, which is particularly good for nice-looking letters, newsletters and the like… in fact, large amounts of the text in this book were drafted using Pages. It's a bit like a stripped-back, user-friendly version of Word, and comes with a wide range of templates to base your projects on. Used in landscape mode the toolbars vanish so you can concentrate on your typing, while in portrait mode a plethora of tools appear at the top. Files can be exported to your Mac or PC via iTunes (see box) in either Pages, PDF or Word formats.

• **Doc² HD** This app is a good alternative to Pages, though nowhere near as polished. The formatting tools are really impressive, offering everything from bold, italic and underline to bulleting, indenting and table construction. Its best feature is the fact that it works with Google Docs to help you share your files online.

• **WordPress** For the WordPress bloggers out there, the iPad app is a must, both well designed and easy to use. As well as creating and editing your posts, you can also use the tool to moderate comments.

• **Split Pea** Combines a text editor with a web browser, which is incredibly useful when you're researching topics online whilst writing, as it saves the need to keep switching back and forth between apps.

• **Bashō** This app (pictured here) offers an iPad-formatted, distraction-free writing environment where you can get on with your writing without toolbars and formatting worries. It works in a white-on-black mode that makes it easy on the eye for extended periods of writing. If you don't get on with this one, check out **WriteRoom**, which does a similar job.

> **Tip:** When searching for **Bashō** in the App Store, it won't show up if you use a regular "o" character. Tap and hold the "o" key until the "ō" option appears, then slide your finger to select it.

Working with numbers

• **Numbers** This iWork application, as already mentioned, is Apple's answer to Excel. Though not as sophisticated as the Microsoft desktop program in terms of advanced spreadsheet features, it is nicely put together, and does an impressive job of creating charts and graphs. The templates are excellent and you can move between dry-looking data and something eye-popping with little effort. The **Export** feature allows you to send files via iTunes as either PDF or in the Numbers format, but not in the Excel format.

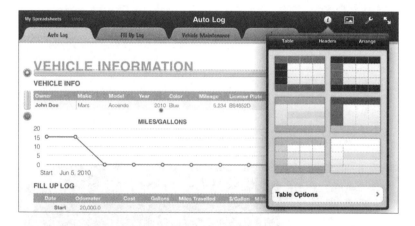

Tip: Documents can also be shared online from iWork apps via the iWork.com website (apple.com/iwork/iwork-dot-com). In any of the three apps, tap the 📧 icon below any file in the document gallery.

• **Sheet² HD** This app can be used to create some pretty impressive spreadsheets and, unlike the iWork Numbers app, it can export files in the Excel format. It also keys in with Google Docs for sharing your files online.

• **PCalc Lite** The iPad does not come with a built-in calculator, but there are dozens of options available in the App Store. PCalc Lite is free, looks nice and boasts some scientific functions.

• **Quick Graph** This free app can be used to produce both 2-D and 3-D graphs from complex formulas and equations.

• **OmniGraphSketcher** Though pricey, OmniGraphSketcher (pictured here) is the best graph and chart building tool available for the iPad. You can import data to build your charts or draw by hand. The elegant results can either be exported via email in the native format or as PDF. You can also copy and paste your creations into the iPad iWork apps.

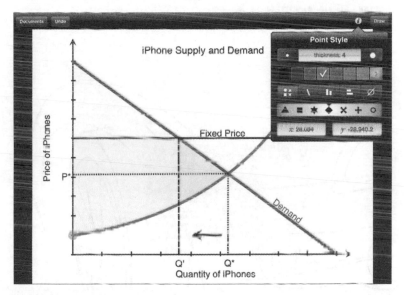

Working with graphics

In the Getting Creative chapter (p.154) there are several recommendations for excellent painting and photo-manipulation apps, but if you're an illustrator, engineer or designer, you might well be after a dedicated CAD/vector drawing app. Here's a few to try:

• **iPocket Draw** With a really nice user interface and loads of tools for creating shapes and lines (complete with support for detailed curve manipulation), this is a fine choice.

• **iDesign** Another very interesting design and illustration tool that really shows off the potential of the iPad's Multi-Touch interface. There are no messy toolbars, as all the controls are called up within a transparent overlay panel (pictured here).

• **iMockups for iPad** For swiftly and efficiently knocking together wire-frame demos of websites, apps, or whatever, this is an essential piece of kit.

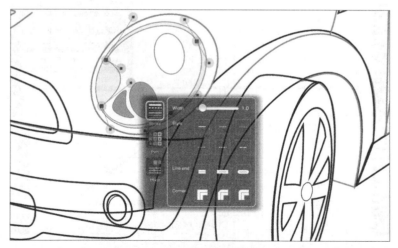

Working with presentations

- **Keynote** The third member of the iWork tool kit (pictured here) is a pared-back, but stylish equivalent of PowerPoint from Microsoft Office. Again, what it lacks in features it makes up for in ease of use and elegant templates. Though it can open and edit PowerPoint documents, it's worth noting that Keynote can only export files in either its own format or as a PDF, which is annoying if you had wanted to get them back into PowerPoint on a desktop machine.

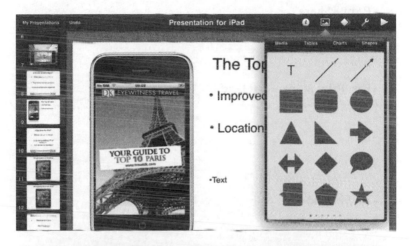

Tip: You can connect your iPad to a projector and use Keynote to run your presentation as well as create it, using an iPad Dock Connector to VGA adapter (see p.248).

- **ProPrompter** With this app you can turn the iPad into a script teleprompter, and with the same app installed on another device (either iPad, iPhone or iPod Touch) you can control the pace of the script on the iPad's screen via a Bluetooth connection.

Printing

Few productivity apps let you print directly from the iPad. You can't print a document from any iWork app at the time of writing, for example, so if you do need a hard copy, you first have to either export the file via the iTunes File Sharing feature (see p.232), email it to yourself, or share it with yourself via iWork.com (see p.234).

There are, however, a few apps that offer some printing functionality...

• **PrinterShare** This software lets you print from the iPad – over the airwaves – photos, contacts' details, webpages, and the contents of the iPad's clipboard (i.e., anything clipped using the **Copy** command). For the full story, visit PrinterShare.com.

• **Fax, Print & Share For iPad** This app does exactly what it says on the tin, working with both network printers and "shared" printers connected to a desktop machine. The fax feature is a useful bonus. It can handle any documents created in iWork apps, and can also be used to wirelessly share files between iPads. The setup process can be a little fiddly, but it's worth the effort.

• **Air Sharing HD** Mentioned elsewhere in this book, this excellent app gives onboard file storage, Wi-Fi file sharing and access to networked printers.

Making notes

Though you could use the word processor packages already discussed for note-taking, there are numerous apps available for the iPad that work hard to help you organize and sync your notes. Here's a few of... er... note.

• **Notes** This is a freebie that you'll find preinstalled on the iPad. Aside from the fact that Apple have failed to provide any alternative fonts to the default Marker Felt, and you get a choice of yellow, yellow or yellow to write on, the app is pretty sound. Arguably its most compelling feature is that notes can be synced with a Mac or PC via iTunes. To do this, connect your iPad, select it in the iTunes sidebar, and check the **Sync notes** box under the **Info** tab.

• **Evernote** Evernote is among the best note-taking tools and services available. The iPad app (pictured here) can create notes from text, images and audio and these notes are then synced between the Evernote server and whatever desktop or mobile versions of Evernote you are running. By far the coolest feature of Evernote is the fact that images you add as notes are uploaded, processed, and then become searchable by any text in the images. While the app will cost you nothing to install, the Evernote service comes in two flavours: a free version, which allows you a monthly upload limit of 40MB; and a premium version that gives you 500MB. Play about with the free version first to get a feel for how quickly you use up your quota. As you might expect, photo notes will swallow your bandwidth pretty fast, while sticking with text notes will stretch your usage allowance further.

• **Bento** This app falls somewhere between being a note-taking tool, a to-do list organizer and a fully featured database management tool (for keeping track of a record collection, say). It looks beautiful, has various themes, and can be used either as a stand-alone app or in conjunction with the Mac desktop version.

• **Penultimate** A really attractive note-taking app designed to be used with your finger acting as a pen. You can't type into it, but it's great for scrawling down shorthand notes or just doodling. You get a choice of graph, lined or plain pages and you can email either pages or whole notebooks. Probably most useful when combined with a stylus such as those made by Pogo (see p.15), as writing with a digit can be quite tricky and tiring.

• **Stick It** A fun way to make notes and lists on the iPad. The results can then be saved and displayed as your iPad's Home Screen (pictured here) or Lock Screen.

Part 12

....

Accessories

Docks, covers and more

A roundup of iPad extras

There's an awful lot of choice out there when it comes to buying accessories for your iPad; and there's also a lot of confusion about which older iPhone and iPod accessories will work with the iPad. As a general rule, assume that any device that came out before 2009 and connects via the Dock Connector isn't going to work. As for what does work, Apple produce a handful of items, but there's lots more besides. In this chapter we take a quick look at a few desirable artefacts and offer up some advice to help you choose.

Docks and stands

iPad Docks are stands with sockets that make it convenient to connect and disconnect the iPad to computers, power sources, TVs, speakers or hi-fis. There is even an Apple Dock with an integrated keyboard. Apple iPad Docks feature a genuine line-out socket for audio connections, as opposed to a headphone socket, so the sound quality is improved when connecting to a hi-fi or speakers.

Several companies are also making stands, though many are poorly conceived and don't really reflect the way that people use the iPad. One worth looking at, however, is the aluminium Macally ViewStand, which is great if you regularly use the iPad to watch movies.

- **Apple iPad Dock** tinyurl.com/appleipaddock

- **Macally ViewStand** tinyurl.com/viewstand

Tip: Also check out the Apple iPad Case and Macally BookStand, mentioned on p.246, both cases that fold in such a way that they work as an iPad stand as well.

Keyboards

Apple produce a special iPad Keyboard Dock so that you can tap away with the iPad mounted in front of you in portrait mode. If you intend to do a lot of typing with the iPad it's probably worth getting, though it does feel odd using a physical keyboard whilst still having to tap away on the screen for other functions.

The regular Apple Wireless Keyboard also works with the iPad, connecting via Bluetooth. As such, you can expect that most other brands of Bluetooth keyboard will also work, though check with the manufacturer before you buy one. To connect a USB keyboard, try using the Apple Camera Connection Kit as intermediary (see p.248).

- **Apple Wireless Keyboard** tinyurl.com/applewirelesskeys

- **Apple iPad Keyboard Dock** tinyurl.com/applekeyboarddock

To set up a Bluetooth keyboard with the iPad, make sure the peripheral is turned on and then, on the iPad, tap **Settings > General > Bluetooth**, toggle Bluetooth on and then wait for the devices to connect.

Covers and cases

There are so many varieties to choose from here. Do you go for a protective shell? Examples of these include the Belkin Grip Swell, which covers the aluminium reverse face of the iPad with rippled rubber, or the Macally METROMPAD, which combines tough clear plastic with a mirrored reverse (like that of an iPod Touch). They are all well and good, but while they can offer pretty colours and extra grip, they can be annoying when you want to connect to a Dock or some other device. Equally, they offer no protection for the screen.

• **Belkin Grip Swell For iPad** tinyurl.com/gripswell

• **Macally METROMPAD** tinyurl.com/metrompad

Whilst we are on the subject of screens, many people are tempted to buy stick-on screen protection films. Though some swear by such products, many long-term iPhone users will tell you that the glass touchscreens are remarkably resilient to scratching, so unless you are particularly accident prone, save your pennies for something else.

Far better is a case that fully encloses the iPad. Many are of the traditional laptop-style (with a zip on one side), such as the Belkin Vue Sleeve, which has a reinforced panel to protect the screen and a transparent pocket for accessories.

• **Belkin Vue Sleeve** tinyurl.com/vuesleeve

Other cases feature a flap that, like a book cover, opens to reveal the iPad's screen. Apple's own iPad case (pictured here) is a good example of one of these and, like the Macally BookStand, doubles as a prop for typing, viewing movies, etc.

- **Apple iPad Case** tinyurl.com/applestoreipadcase

- **Macally BookStand** tinyurl.com/macallybookstand

Headphones

As you might expect, the iPad's headphone socket will work with any headphones with a standard quarter-inch minijack plug. It's also worth noting that many brands that feature play controls on the cord (such as the Apple In-Ear Headphones) will enable you to control certain **iPod** and **Videos** app playback features. Shure SE series headphones are also excellent, while the Shure MPA adapter lead can be used to add playback controls.

Product reviews

All Apple Store (store.apple.com) pages feature customer reviews, which can be an invaluable source of information, even if you don't end up buying the goods from Apple. Here are a few review and tech sites that are also worth looking at when choosing iPad extras (and when looking for iPad news in general):

- **iLounge** ilounge.com/index.php/accessories

- **Engadget** engadget.com

- **Slash Gear** slashgear.com

- **Obama Pacman** obamapacman.com

Though it's worth checking with the manufacturer before you buy, you should also be able to pair any Bluetooth headphones with an iPad via the options within Settings > General > Bluetooth.

- **Apple Headphones** apple.com/ipod/in-ear-headphones

- **Shure SE Series and MPA adapter** store.shure.com

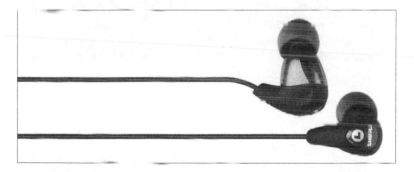

Miscellaneous

• **Apple iPad 10W power adapter** (tinyurl.com/ipad10wpower) You get one of these adapters in the box with the iPad, but they are incredibly useful (especially given that iPads can be picky about what they charge from, see p.93), so you might want to invest in another to take out and about with you. It connects to the iPad via a USB Dock Connector cable. There are other, cheaper, non-Apple USB power adapters on the market, but be sure to check that they supply the necessary 10W of power before you buy.

• **Apple iPad Dock Connector to VGA Adapter** (tinyurl.com/ipadvga) You use this device to connect an iPad to a TV, projector or VGA monitor. It's especially useful if you intend to connect to a projector to show a Keynote presentation. You will also need a standard VGA cable to connect the adapter to the TV, projector or monitor.

• **Apple iPad Camera Connection Kit** (tinyurl.com/ipadcamkit) Also worth a look is this two-part kit. You get two Dock Connector adapters: one for reading image files from digital camera SD cards, and another for connecting cameras (and iPhones) via a USB cable to download images (see p.148).

> **Tip:** You can use the USB device from the Camera Connection Kit to connect USB headsets (for making Skype calls perhaps, see p.20) and also many USB keyboards.

Index

A

AAC   121, 144

ABC Player   138

accent characters, typing   73

accessibility settings   80

AccuRadio   132

Address Book (Mac)   181

Adobe Digital Editions   113

Adobe Flash   42, 194, 198

Adobe InDesign   113

AIFF   121

AIM   177

Air Harp   133

Air Mouse   31

Airport Express   131

Air Sharing HD   30, 232, 238

Alarm! HD   192

AnyDVD   122

AOL   140, 158

Aperture (Mac)   147

Apple A4 chip   36

AppleCare   39, 53

Apple ID   61, 140

Apple Insider   56

Apple Lossless   121

Apple Newton   11

Apple Remote   131

Apple TV   131

apps settings 100

apps syncing   100

At Bat 2010   138

Audible   121

audiobook playback   130

audio syncing   63

authorizing computers for iTunes   99, 144

auto-correct   75

auto-lock settings   66

AV Cables   136

B

backups   91

Bashō   233

battery charge cycles   92

battery life, maximizing   92

battery replacement   38

BBC News   211

Beejive   177

Bento   240

bitrates   121

Bluetooth   20, 87, 181, 182

Bluetooth headphones   247

Bluetooth keyboards   244

Boingo   83

bookmark syncing   43, 200

bookmarking in iBooks   109

Boxee   138

Brushes   154

buying an iPad   46, 50

buying a used iPad   53, 54

C

CAD   236

calculator   235

CalDAV   185

calendar settings   191

calendar syncing   62, 161, 182

Camera Connection Kit   148, 248

Camera For iPad   87, 149

caps lock   74